Excel® 2007
FOR
DUMMIES®
QUICK REFERENCE

by John Walkenbach and Colin Banfield

BICENTENNIAL
1807
WILEY
2007
BICENTENNIAL

Wiley Publishing, Inc.

Excel® 2007 For Dummies® Quick Reference

Published by
Wiley Publishing, Inc.
111 River Street
Hoboken, NJ 07030-5774

www.wiley.com

Copyright © 2007 by Wiley Publishing, Inc., Indianapolis, Indiana

Published by Wiley Publishing, Inc., Indianapolis, Indiana

Published simultaneously in Canada

For general information on our other products and services, please contact our Customer Care Department within the U.S. at 800-762-2974, outside the U.S. at 317-572-3993, or fax 317-572-4002.

For technical support, please visit www.wiley.com/techsupport.

Wiley also publishes its books in a variety of electronic formats. Some content that appears in print may not be available in electronic books.

Library of Congress Control Number: 2006934839

ISBN-13: 978-0-470-04671-5

ISBN-10: 0-470-04671-6

Manufactured in the United States of America

10 9 8 7 6 5 4 3 2

1O/RT/RS/QW/IN

WILEY

About the Authors

John Walkenbach is a leading authority on spreadsheet software and is principal of JWalk and Associates Inc., a small San Diego–based consulting firm that specializes in spreadsheet application development. He is the author of approximately three dozen spreadsheet books and has written hundreds of articles and reviews for a variety of publications, including *PC World*, *InfoWorld*, *Windows* magazine, and *PC/Computing*. John graduated from the University of Missouri and earned a master's and a PhD from the University of Montana. Visit his Web site at www.j-walk.com.

Colin Banfield has been working in the telecommunications field for more than twenty-five years and has been using spreadsheet programs for more than two decades. Colin's largest Excel project to date is a comprehensive tool that is designed for telephone central office equipment configuration, pricing, and manufacturing and used by sales, engineering, and manufacturing personnel. In between his telecom consulting duties, Colin works with organizations to extract information from corporate databases for business intelligence reporting in Excel. In his spare time, Colin writes and reviews books for Wiley and enjoys photography, astronomy, and expanding his musical repertoire. Colin holds a BSc (Honors) in Electrical Engineering from the University of the West Indies and has received extensive training in many advanced technologies.

Dedication

To Dorothy, my most loving and patient better half, and one of the nicest people on the planet. —C. B.

Author's Acknowledgments

Thanks to the folks at Wiley who helped with the update of this book. In particular, my project editor, Susan Pink (Pinkie to me), did her usual wonderful editing and coordinating job and kept me on my toes. I'm indebted to Allen Wyatt, who provided a thorough technical review and made some very good suggestions for improvement. Finally, I'd like to thank David Gainer, Lead Program Manager for Excel at Microsoft, and his staff for clarifying some issues and for delivering this amazing update to a superb piece of software. —C. B.

Publisher's Acknowledgments

We're proud of this book; please send us your comments through our online registration form located at www.dummies.com/register/.

Some of the people who helped bring this book to market include the following:

Acquisitions, Editorial, and Media Development

Project Editor: Susan Pink

(Previous Edition: Christine Berman)

Acquisitions Editor: Greg Croy

Copy Editor: Susan Pink

(Previous Edition: John Edwards)

Technical Editor: Allen Wyatt

Editorial Manager: Jodi Jensen

Media Development Manager: Laura VanWinkle

Editorial Assistant: Amanda Foxworth

Composition Services

Project Coordinator: Heather Kolter, Ryan Steffen

Layout and Graphics: Stephanie D. Jumper, Barry Offringa, Lynsey Osborn, Heather Ryan

Proofreaders: Dwight Ramsey, Evelyn Still, Brian H. Walls

Indexer: Techbooks

Publishing and Editorial for Technology Dummies

    Richard Swadley, Vice President and Executive Group Publisher

    Andy Cummings, Vice President and Publisher

    Mary Bednarek, Executive Acquisitions Director

    Mary C. Corder, Editorial Director

Publishing for Consumer Dummies

    Diane Graves Steele, Vice President and Publisher

    Joyce Pepple, Acquisitions Director

Composition Services

    Gerry Fahey, Vice President of Production Services

    Debbie Stailey, Director of Composition Services

Contents at a Glance

Table of Contents

Part 1

Getting to Know Excel 2007

With Microsoft's popular Excel 2007 spreadsheet program, you can enter, manipulate, and analyze data in ways that would be impossible, cumbersome, or error prone for you to do manually. This part gives you the basics you need to get up and running quickly in Excel.

In this part . . .

- ✓ Familiarizing Yourself with the Excel 2007 Window
- ✓ Navigating with the Mouse and Keyboard
- ✓ Introducing the Ribbon, Quick Access Toolbar, and Office Menu
- ✓ Formatting with Themes and Previewing Your Formatting Live

Excel Basics

Excel documents are known as *workbooks*. A single workbook can store as many sheets as will fit into memory, and these sheets are stacked like the pages in a notebook. Sheets can be either *worksheets* (a normal spreadsheet-type sheet with rows and columns) or *chart sheets* (a special sheet that holds a single chart).

Most of the time, you perform tasks in worksheets. In older versions of Excel (well, except for really old versions), each worksheet used a grid with 65,536 rows and 256 columns. Excel numbers rows starting with 1 and assigns letters to columns starting with A. After Excel exhausts the letters of the alphabet, column lettering continues with AA, AB, and so on. So column 1 is A, column 26 is Z, column 27 is AA, column 52 is AZ, column 53 is BA, and so on. Prior to Excel 2007, row numbers ranged from 1 to 65,536 and column labels ranged from A (column 1) to IV (column 256).

Excel 2007 increases the number of rows and columns in a single worksheet significantly. A worksheet now has 1,048,576 rows (no, that's not a typo) and 16,384 columns (no, that's not a typo either). Rows are numbered from 1 to 1048576 and columns are labeled from A to XFD.

The intersection of a row and a column is called a *cell*. A quick calculation using Excel tells me that this works out to 17,179,869,184 cells — more than enough for just about any use. Cells have *addresses,* which are based on their row and column. The upper-left cell in a worksheet is called A1, and the cell down at the bottom right is called XFD1048576. Cell K9 (also known as the dog cell) is the intersection of the eleventh column and the ninth row.

You might be wondering about the amount of system memory (known as random access memory, or RAM) you need to accommodate all those rows and columns. The actual memory you need depends on the amount of data you store in the workbook and the number of open workbooks. The good news is that Excel 2007 allows you to work with more memory than previous versions. Excel 2003, for example, will utilize up to only 1 GB (gigabyte) of memory, even if your system has more memory available. In Excel 2007, the memory available is limited by the maximum amount of memory that your version of Windows (XP or Vista) can use.

Formulas

A cell in Excel can hold a number, some text, a formula, or nothing at all. You already know what numbers and text are, but you may be a bit fuzzy on the concept of a formula. A *formula* tells Excel to perform a calculation using information stored in other cells. For example, you can insert a formula that tells Excel to add the values in the first 10 cells in column A and to display the result in the cell that contains the formula.

Formulas can use normal arithmetic operators such as + (plus), — (minus), * (multiply), and / (divide). They can also use special built-in functions that let you do powerful things without much effort on your part. For example, Excel has functions that add a range of values, calculate square roots, compute loan payments, and even tell you the time of day. Part 5 covers how to use the various functions in Excel.

Active cell and ranges

In Excel, one of the cells in a worksheet is always the active cell. The *active cell* is the one that's selected, and it's displayed with a thicker border than the others. Its contents appear in the *formula bar*. You can select a group, or *range*, of cells by clicking and dragging the mouse pointer over them. You can then issue a command that does something to the active cell or to the range.

The selected range is usually a group of contiguous cells, but it doesn't have to be. To select a noncontiguous group of cells, select the first cell or group of cells, hold down the Ctrl key while you drag the mouse, and select the next cell or group of cells.

Familiarizing Yourself with the Excel 2007 Window

Figure 1-1 shows a typical Excel 2007 window, with the important parts labeled. This terminology rears its ugly head throughout the book, so look at the figure carefully.

Moving, resizing, and closing windows

When Excel and workbook windows are in a *restored* state (between a maximized and minimized state, that is) you can use the resize handles to adjust the window size to your liking. Move the mouse pointer to the area of the resize handle until the pointer changes to a double-headed arrow, and then drag with the mouse.

You can move the window around the screen by dragging the title bars. *See also* "Using the Mouse and Keyboard," later in this part.

When the active workbook window is maximized, it shares a single Close button with the Excel window. After you click the shared Close button, Excel closes the active workbook.

Exiting Excel

Use any one of the following methods to close the Excel application:

- ✔ Click the Close button on the Excel title bar if one or no workbook is open.

- ✔ Click the Office button and then click the Exit Excel button.

✔ Double-click the Office button. **_See_** "Introducing the Office Menu," later in this part.

✔ Press the Alt key, then press F, and then press X.

Select all button

Control button

Office button   Mouse pointer   Split box

Name box   Formula bar   Help

Quick Access toolbar   Excel title bar   Close

Active   Workbook title bar   Maximize/Restore
cell   Column
pointer   header   Workbook window   Minimize

Figure 1-1

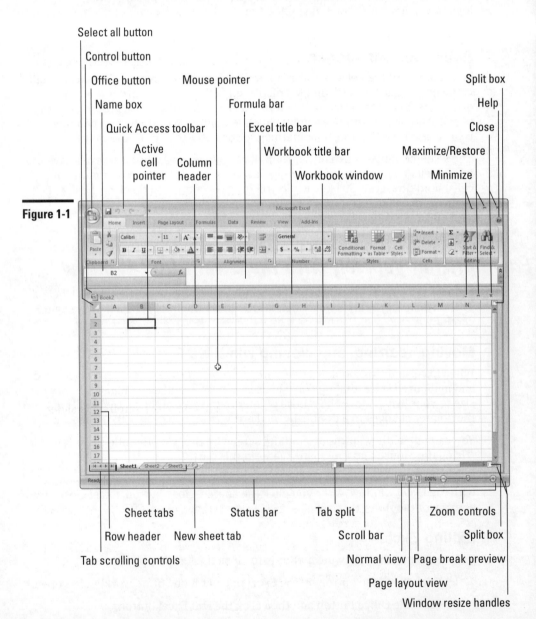

Sheet tabs   Status bar   Tab split   Zoom controls

Row header   New sheet tab   Scroll bar   Split box

Tab scrolling controls   Normal view │ Page break preview

Page layout view

Window resize handles

Navigating with the Mouse and Keyboard

The mouse is the primary tool that you use in Excel for executing commands, making selections, and navigating in the worksheet. Following are the mouse conventions that we use in this book:

- ✓ **Click:** Click the left mouse button once.

- ✓ **Double-click:** Click the left mouse button twice in quick succession. It may take you some time to get the hang of this action.

- ✓ **Right-click:** Click the right mouse button once.

- ✓ **Drag:** Hold down the left mouse button and move the mouse. Release the mouse button to complete the drag operation.

- ✓ **Hover:** Place the mouse pointer over an element without clicking a mouse button.

- ✓ **Select:** Place the mouse pointer over an element and click the left mouse button.

Mousing around

Every mouse action is associated with some element in the Excel window. An *element* can be a slider, button, cell, chart object, and so on. You select or hover over the element using the mouse pointer.

Navigating through a worksheet with a mouse works just as you'd expect. Just click a cell, and it becomes the active cell. If the cell that you want to activate isn't visible in the workbook window, you can use the scroll bars to scroll the window in any direction, as follows:

- ✓ To scroll one cell, click one of the arrows on the scroll bar.

- ✓ To scroll by a complete screen, click either side of the scroll bar's slider button (the large center button).

- ✓ To scroll faster, drag the slider.

- ✓ To scroll a long distance vertically, press and hold the Shift key while dragging the slider button.

Note that only the active workbook window displays scroll bars. If you activate a different window, its scroll bars appear.

After you right-click a cell, a range of cells, or another object in the worksheet area, Excel displays a *contextual* menu, so-called because the menu includes commands specific to working with the cell, range, or object.

For your convenience, Excel 2007 adds a mini-toolbar above the contextual menu with useful commands drawn from the Ribbon, as shown in Figure 1-2. **See also** "Introducing the Ribbon," later in this part.

Figure 1-2

Using the keyboard

Most users will be comfortable using the mouse to do all their work in Excel. For users who prefer to use the keyboard exclusively when working in Windows applications or for users who prefer to split the use of the mouse and keyboard among various tasks, Excel provides the following solutions.

- ✔ Keyboard shortcuts
- ✔ Keyboard navigation
- ✔ KeyTips

The first two functions are described next. For more on the last function, KeyTips, **see** "Tipping off your keyboard," later in this part.

You can access commands in Excel using *keyboard shortcuts,* which are individual keystrokes or a combination of keys pressed simultaneously. To access the Print command using a shortcut, for example, you press and hold down the Ctrl key and press the P key, represented in this book as Ctrl+P. The following table lists some common keyboard shortcuts in Excel.

Shortcut	*Action*
Ctrl+A	Select all
Ctrl+B	Apply or remove bold formatting
Ctrl+C	Copy selection

Shortcut	*Action*
Ctrl+F	Find
Ctrl+G or F5	Go To
Ctrl+H	Replace
Ctrl+I	Apply or remove italic formatting
Ctrl+O or Ctrl+F12	Open a document
Ctrl+P	Print
Ctrl+S or Shift+F12	Save
Ctrl+U	Apply or remove underlining
Ctrl+V	Paste
Ctrl+W or Ctrl+F4	Close the active workbook
Crtl+X	Cut
Ctrl+Y or F4	Repeat the last action
Ctrl+Z	Undo the last action
F1	Display the help viewer
Ctrl+F1	Hide or display the Ribbon commands
F2	Enable editing within the active cell

With more than 17 billion cells in a worksheet, you need ways to move to specific cells. Fortunately, Excel provides you with many techniques to move around a worksheet. As always, you can use either your mouse or the keyboard on your navigational journeys. The following table lists the keystrokes that enable you to move through a worksheet.

Keys	*Action*
Up arrow	Moves the active cell one row up
Down arrow	Moves the active cell one row down
Left arrow	Moves the active cell one column to the left
Right arrow	Moves the active cell one column to the right
PgUp	Moves the active cell one screen up
PgDn	Moves the active cell one screen down
Alt+PgDn	Moves the active cell one screen right
Alt+PgUp	Moves the active cell one screen left
Home	Moves the active cell to the first column of the row that the active cell is currently in

cont.

Keys	Action
Ctrl+Home	Moves the active cell to the beginning of worksheet (A1)
F5	Displays the Go To dialog box
Ctrl+Backspace	Scrolls the screen to display the active cell
Up arrow*	Scrolls the screen one row up (active cell doesn't change)
Down arrow*	Scrolls the screen one row down (active cell doesn't change)
Left arrow*	Scrolls the screen one column left (active cell doesn't change)
Right arrow*	Scrolls the screen one column right (active cell doesn't change)

* With Scroll Lock on

Introducing the Ribbon

Excel 2007 comes with a new user interface that replaces the standard menus and toolbars found at the top of the window in previous versions of Excel. The new interface is called the *Ribbon* and consists of a series of tabs, each containing a variety of commands grouped according to function (see Figure 1-3). Virtually all the features in Excel 2007 are available through the commands in the Ribbon tabs. This arrangement allows you to discover features in the program far more easily than if you had to drill down several layers into menus.

Figure 1-3

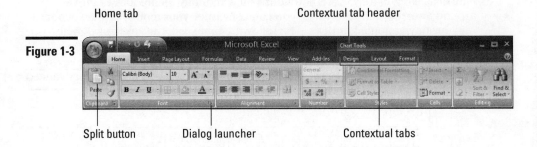

Home tab   Contextual tab header

Split button   Dialog launcher   Contextual tabs

Dissecting the parts of the Ribbon

The commands in the Ribbon are accessed through a variety of *controls*. Here's a list of the various types of controls and other parts that make up the Ribbon:

- **Button:** This is the most common type of control. Most buttons in the Ribbon (except the formatting ones) have descriptive text associated with them, so you don't need to be a Mensa expert to figure out what a button represents. The most frequently used commands in each Ribbon tab have larger buttons.

Most buttons execute commands directly when you click them. However, some buttons have a built-in downward-pointing arrow, and others have an attached downward-pointing arrow. Clicking a button with a built-in arrow displays a menu or gallery. For a button with an attached arrow (known as a *split button*), the icon part of the button represents the most common command for the button. Clicking the arrow part displays a menu with additional command choices. The two types of buttons with arrows look similar but if you hover the mouse pointer over a button with an attached arrow, you see a clear delineation between the icon (command) part and the arrow (menu) part (see Figure 1-3).

✔ **Check box:** A square box that you click to turn an option on or off.

✔ **Command group:** Each Ribbon tab contains groups of related commands. For example, you find commands related to text fonts in the Fonts group of the Home tab.

✔ **Dialog launcher:** A command that launches a dialog box (a pop-up window) from within a command group, menu, or gallery. The dialog launcher in a command group is a little button in the bottom right of the group. In addition, some menus and galleries contain options that launch dialog boxes. After you click a dialog launcher, a dialog box appears that presents additional choices. (However, the Ribbon displays the commands you are likely to use frequently, thus minimizing the need to launch dialog boxes.)

✔ **Drop-down list:** A list of things you can choose from. Click the control's downward-pointing arrow to display the list.

✔ **Gallery:** A *gallery* is a new control in Excel 2007 that presents you with a set of graphic choices, such as a particular formatting style (patterns, colors, and effects) or a predefined layout. An example of a predefined layout is a chart choice with specific elements preselected for inclusion in the chart. Galleries enable Excel to be more results oriented; that is, they present the likely result you are looking for first and then expose advanced choices through a dialog box or Ribbon command.

Three types of galleries are available:

- **Drop-down gallery:** This is displayed after you click a button with a downward-pointing arrow. This type of gallery presents a single column of choices and includes both graphic and text elements.

- **Drop-down grid:** This is displayed after you click a button with a downward-pointing arrow. This type of gallery presents a two-dimensional grid of choices and does not include text.

- **In-Ribbon gallery:** Like the drop-down grid, but this gallery exposes a single row of choices directly within a Ribbon control group. You can click up and down scroll arrows to reveal additional rows, or you can click a drop-down arrow to display the full set of choices in a two-dimensional grid.

✔ **Help button:** On the far right of the Ribbon is the help button (the question mark). Click this button for general Excel help.

✔ **Menu, rich:** Rich menus are new in Excel 2007. Each menu choice has an illustrative graphic, the command name, and in some cases a short description of what the command does.

TIP

Don't confuse rich menus with drop-down galleries, although they look similar. Menus contain related commands. Galleries allow you to choose from among a set of formats or layouts.

✔ **Menu, standard:** Most users are already familiar with this form of menu — a drop-down list of choices with command names (such as Paste or Insert Cells). Some command names have small associated icons. If you click a command name that ends with an ellipsis (...), Excel displays a dialog box that presents further choices.

✔ **Spinner:** A control with two arrows (one pointing up, the other pointing down) used with an input box to specify a number (height or width, for example.) Clicking an arrow increases or decreases the number in the input box. You can also enter a number in the box directly. The spinner control allows you to use only valid numbers.

✔ **Tab, contextual:** Contextual tabs give the Ribbon the power to expose all features in Excel. One or more contextual tabs appear after you insert or select an object, such as a chart, shape, table, or picture. For example, after you insert a chart, three contextual tabs related to chart functionality appear on the Ribbon and a header labeled Chart Tools appears on the Excel title bar above the contextual tabs. Contextual tabs contain all the commands you need for working with the particular object. After you deselect an object, the contextual tabs (and the header) disappear.

The general rules that govern the display of contextual tabs follow:

- After you select an object (such as a chart, shape, or table), one or more contextual tabs for the object appear on the Ribbon. You must select a tab to display the associated commands.

- After you insert an object, Excel displays the commands for the first tab of the contextual tab set for that object.

- After you double-click an object, Excel displays the commands for the first tab of the contextual tab set for that object. Note that not all objects have this double-click capability.

- After you select, deselect, and then reselect the object without using any other commands in-between, Excel displays the commands for the first tab of the contextual tab set for that object.

✔ **Tab, standard:** The Ribbon comes with a set of standard tabs, each organized according to the functions of the commands that it contains. For example, the Insert tab contains command groups to insert shapes, charts, tables, pictures, and so on. An exception is the Home tab, which is so-named because this is where you do most of your work in Excel.

If your mouse has a scroll wheel, you can navigate quickly among the Ribbon tabs by hovering the mouse pointer over the Ribbon area and scrolling the wheel back and forth.

✔ **Text box:** A box in which you enter a number or text. In general, the Ribbon associates a text box with another control, such as a spinner or a drop-down box.

Sizing up the Ribbon

The layout of the Ribbon controls is not static. Depending on your screen resolution, or the Excel window size, or both, the Ribbon provides one of four layout options for command groups. If sufficient space is available, the Ribbon presents a layout that labels commands, displays more commands individually, and eliminates extra clicks. As you resize the Ribbon downwards (by reducing the screen resolution or shrinking the size of the Excel window), the Ribbon rearranges the layout of some of the command groups by first resizing command buttons (larger buttons become smaller), then removing labels from commands, and finally reducing the groups to single large buttons (see Figure 1-4). To access the commands in a command group that the Ribbon resizes to a single button, you must first click the button to display a flyout menu and then select the command.

Figure 1-4

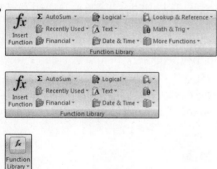

It is important to note that at each stage of downward resizing, no command groups or commands disappear entirely from the Ribbon. The multiple layout options for the command groups ensure that nothing is lost as space becomes more limited. If you reduce the size of the Excel window sufficiently, however, the Ribbon disappears altogether.

Tipping off your keyboard

Excel provides a feature called KeyTips that allow you to access every command on the Ribbon using the keyboard, without having to memorize keystroke combinations! So, what are KeyTips? *KeyTips* are little alphanumerical indicators containing a single letter, a combination of two letters, or a number, indicating what to type to activate the command under them, as shown in Figure 1-5.

Figure 1-5

Follow these steps to access a command in a Ribbon tab using a KeyTip:

1. Press the Alt key. The KeyTips appear over the Ribbon tabs (Ignore the KeyTips that appear in the other areas of the interface for this exercise.)

2. Press the key that represents the KeyTip for the Ribbon tab you want to access. For example, press N to select the Insert tab. Note that you *do not* have to hold down the Alt key. If you need to select a different tab after you select the KeyTip for a tab, press the Esc key.

3. Press the key or key combination that represents the KeyTip for the command you want to use.

If the command you select is a drop-down gallery or drop-down grid, you can use an arrow key or the Tab key to highlight your choice and then press the Enter key to select your choice.

Remember: KeyTips are associated with in-Ribbon galleries, so you have to press the key that represents the KeyTip for the gallery before you can choose an option in the gallery.

Remember: If the command you want to use requires a number key, you must use the number keys on the main keyboard. The KeyTip feature does not work with the numeric keypad.

Hiding the Ribbon commands

If you find that the Ribbon commands take up too much of your screen area, you can hide them using any of the following methods:

✔ Press Ctrl+F1

✔ Double-click any Ribbon tab

✔ Right-click in the Ribbon area and choose Minimize the Ribbon from the contextual menu

✔ Click the arrow to the right of the Quick Access toolbar and choose Minimize the Ribbon from the menu

If you click a tab after you hide the Ribbon commands, Excel displays the tab commands temporarily. The command display is hidden again after you select a command in the tab or click away from the Ribbon area. Similarly, you can use KeyTips to select a command when the command display is hidden.

To redisplay the commands permanently after you hide them, use the same methods described for hiding the commands.

Remember: Excel maintains the hidden condition of the Ribbon commands if you exit and subsequently re-launch Excel.

Introducing the Quick Access Toolbar

The Quick Access toolbar is an area of the new user interface that provides quick access to commands. The toolbar is designed to reduce the amount of navigation you have to do in the Ribbon to access the features that you use frequently. The Quick Access toolbar is on the left side of the screen, above the Ribbon and to the right of the Office button (see Figure 1-6).

Figure 1-6

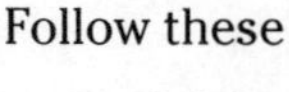

The Quick Access toolbar is the only area of the new user interface that you can customize by adding commands to the three default commands (Save, Undo, and Redo).

Follow these steps to add a command to the toolbar:

1. Select the Ribbon tab that houses the command you want to add.

2. Right-click the command and choose Add to Quick Access Toolbar in the menu that appears.

To quickly add some common commands to the Quick Access toolbar, click the arrow to the right of the toolbar and choose a command from the menu.

You can add an entire command group to the Quick Access toolbar. Just right-click an area in the command group name (for example, Font) and choose Add to Quick Access Toolbar.

Follow these steps to remove a command (including the default commands) from the toolbar:

1. Right-click the command you want to remove from the toolbar.

2. Choose Remove from Quick Access Toolbar in the menu that appears.

 If you think you'll be adding a lot of commands to the Quick Access toolbar, it's a good idea to move the toolbar from the title bar to a separate location below the Ribbon. Right-click anywhere on the toolbar and choose Place Quick Access Toolbar below the Ribbon in the menu that appears. You can regain screen area for working in the worksheet by double-clicking a Ribbon tab (or pressing Ctrl+F1) to hide the Ribbon controls temporarily.

You can access commands on the Quick Access toolbar using the keyboard. Press the Alt key and then a number key that represents the KeyTip for the command you want to access. **See also** "Tipping off your keyboard," earlier in this part.

Introducing the Office Menu

 Excel 2007 introduces a new menu for working with documents and accessing special Excel options. The menu is accessed by clicking the Office button (the large round button with the Office logo), located at the top-left corner of the Excel screen. See Figure 1-7.

Figure 1-7

The menu is divided into two sections. The left section contains a list of document-related commands. By default, the right section displays a list of recently used documents. Click a document name in the list to open the file. Click a pushpin to the right of a document name to keep the document on the list permanently. By default, Excel lists 17 documents, which get overridden with new documents unless you use the pushpin control. Some file commands on the left section include a built-in or attached arrow. If you hover the mouse pointer over a command with an attached arrow, you will see a clear demarcation between the button and the arrow. Clicking a button with a built-in arrow or the arrow portion of a button with an attached arrow displays additional choices in the right section of the menu.

The Office menu also includes a button to access various Excel options and a button to exit Excel. We encourage you to visit the options from time to time, because you may find useful application, workbook, or worksheet options that you want to turn on or off. An option in the Advanced section of the Excel Options dialog box, for example, allows you to increase the number of documents displayed in the Recent Documents list to a maximum of 50.

Previewing Your Formatting Live

New in Excel 2007 is a Live Preview feature. When you hover over a formatting option with the mouse pointer, Excel lets you see the effect that the formatting option will have on your selection *before* you commit to applying the option. Your selection might be a cell, range of cells, chart, table, shape, and more.

Suppose that you want to change the font of some text in a cell. In the Ribbon, a drop-down box called the font picker presents a list of available fonts. As you hover over each choice in the font picker, your cell updates to show you what the text would look like if you chose that font. Live Preview avoids the normal tedium of committing to an option, then undoing the option because the result is not what you wanted, and then committing to another option, only to realize that you don't like the new result either, and so on.

You will find Live Preview options throughout Excel in places where formatting alternatives are available — most notably in galleries.

Formatting with Themes

In Excel 2007, you can now use a formatting concept known as a *theme*. A *theme* consists of a combination of fonts, colors, and effects that provide a consistent look among your workbook's elements, including cells, charts, tables, and PivotTables. You apply the theme's fonts, colors, and effects through individual options or the style galleries of the various elements.

Excel applies a default theme to all new workbooks along with a theme gallery so that you can change the default theme. After you select a new theme, all galleries and all the elements in your workbook formatted with theme styles change to match the new theme.

Following is a description of the three parts of a theme:

✔ **Theme font:** A theme uses two complementary fonts — a header font and a body font. All elements using themed styles thus use the same font or fonts. Click the arrow on the drop-down box (called the *font picker*) in the Ribbon's Home tab to see the fonts used in the theme currently applied to the workbook.

✔ **Theme color:** A theme uses a matched set of twelve colors. Click the arrow on the Fill Color or Font Color tool in the Font group of the Home tab to see ten of the colors used in the theme currently applied to the workbook (see Figure 1-8).

Figure 1-8

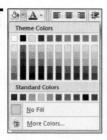

The following are characteristics of theme colors:

• The top row in a color picker displays the base theme colors, and the next five rows display various tints and shades of the base colors. Below the theme colors are standard colors that do not change if the theme is changed. If you want to apply specific formatting that doesn't change after you change the theme, use a standard color.

• The first four colors on the picker (from the left), are intended for text and background use. These colors are designed so that light text always shows well on a dark background, and vice versa.

• The next six colors are used for accents. Most of the theme-style galleries in Excel make extensive use of accent colors.

The two colors that are not exposed on the color pickers are used for hyperlinks (not discussed in this book).

✔ **Theme effect:** Theme effects apply to graphic elements such as charts and shapes and include three levels of styles for outlines, fills, and special effects. Special effects include shadow, glow, bevel, and reflection.

You can change the theme in a workbook by clicking the Themes button in the Ribbon's Page Layout tab and selecting a new theme from the gallery that appears.

Remember: The three Microsoft Office applications — Excel 2007, Word 2007, and PowerPoint 2007 — share the same themes. If you create reports that combine elements from each application, your reports will have a consistent look if you use a common theme.

Soliciting Help

With so many features and options available in Excel, it isn't unusual to get stuck once in a while. Fortunately, Excel provides the following methods for getting help easily:

✔ **Enhanced ScreenTips:** Standard ScreenTips (also called ToolTips) have been available in Excel for some time and provide textual context to commands. After you hover your mouse pointer over a command in earlier versions of Excel, Excel displays the action of the command using either a single word (such as *Paste*) or a brief phrase (such as *Increase Font Size*). A standard ScreenTip helps to decipher the meaning of a command button, for example, when the button has no associated text and the command meaning is unclear from the button icon.

Enhanced ScreenTips take the concept a step further by adding a short description explaining the purpose of the command (hence the prefix *Enhanced*). Some Enhanced ScreenTips include an explanatory graphic when a text description is insufficient to explain the meaning of the command. Enhanced ScreenTips are available for all commands on the Ribbon. In many cases, the ScreenTip explanation provides enough information, so you don't have to seek additional help. By default, Excel 2007 uses Enhanced ScreenTips for all commands.

✔ **Contextual help:** If the Enhanced ScreenTip doesn't offer enough for you to understand the use of a specific command, you can get more detailed help. After you hover the mouse pointer over the command, the Enhanced ScreenTip that pops up lets you know whether additional help for the command is available by indicating that you can press F1 for more help.

If you are in a dialog box and need help for the dialog box options, press the help button (the question mark) to get contextual help.

✔ **General help:** Click the help button (the question mark) on the right side of the Ribbon or press F1 when you are not in a specific context (for example, the mouse pointer is not hovering over a command in the Ribbon) to display a list of general help topics.

When you use contextual help or general help, Excel displays the help viewer, shown in Figure 1-9. The viewer sports Internet browser-style controls. In fact, it was built using the same technology that Microsoft uses in its Internet Explorer browser application. Of course, the viewer is not a full-fledged browser because you can view only Excel help content.

Figure 1-9

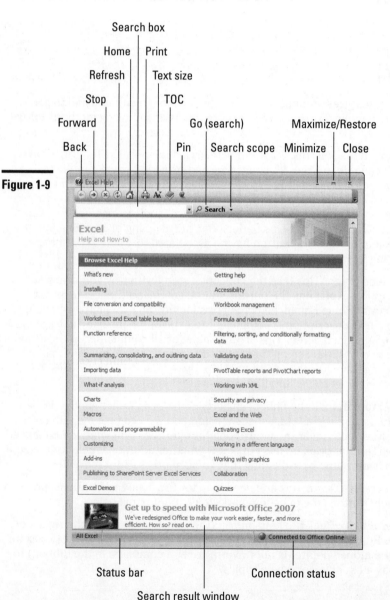

The major features of the help viewer follow:

- ✓ **Search box:** You can enter specific search text in this box. The viewer stores a list of your text searches for the current help session. Click the drop-down arrow on the side of the box to view and select an item from the list if you want to review a previous search result.

- ✓ **Search button:** Click the Search button (or press Enter) to initiate a search after you enter the search text in the search box. Click the arrow next to the search button to define the search scope. By default, if your computer is connected to the Internet, Excel will display help content from an online source. If possible, you should use this source as your first choice because Microsoft updates the contents of online help regularly.

  If you are offline when you initiate a search, Excel uses help content internal to your system. You can force Excel to use internal help content always by clicking the arrow next to the Search button and choosing Offline Excel Help from the menu.

  Whether online or offline, you can narrow you search scope further by selecting an appropriate option from the Search button menu.

- ✓ **Search result window:** This window displays the results of your search request. If you use contextual help or enter text in the search box, the window displays help information specific to the context of the search. If you use general help, the window displays a list of general help topics in the form of titled links. Clicking a link displays a new set of links with more specific titles. Click the specific link title that best matches your search criterion to display detailed information on the topic.

- ✓ **Status bar:** The left side of the status bar (located at the bottom of the help viewer) displays the current search scope. The right side of the status bar displays the connection status. You can click in the connection status area to switch quickly between viewing online and offline help content.

- ✓ **Maximize/Restore button**: Click this button for a full-screen view of the help window. Click again to restore the window to its previous size.

- ✓ **Minimize button:** Click this button to hide the help viewer window. Click the Help button on the Windows taskbar (normally located below the Excel window) to redisplay the viewer.

- ✓ **Close button:** Click this button to close the help viewer.

- ✓ **Pin button:** By default, Excel keeps the help viewer window on top when you are working in the application. Use the Pin button to control this behavior. If you "unpin" the viewer, Excel hides the window automatically if you click anywhere inside the Excel window.

- **TOC (Table of Contents) button:** Click this button to display a Table of Contents pane on the left side of the help viewer. The pane displays the same list of topics that the main windows displays after you select general help or click the Home button. Clicking a main topic in the pane displays a list of subtopics, similar to the subtopics that the main windows displays after you click a general help topic link. The Table of Contents pane is convenient if you want to view the details of multiple subtopics in succession.

- **Text size button:** Click this button to select a size for the text in the search result window.

- **Print button:** Click this button to print the help topic that the search result window displays.

- **Home button:** After browsing multiple helps topics in the search result window, you might want to return to the list of main help topics to choose another general topic link. Click the Home button to return to the list of main help topics.

- **Refresh button:** Click this button to refresh the help topic list after you connect or disconnect from the Internet while the help viewer is open.

- **Stop button:** Click this button to cancel a search request if the help viewer is experiencing difficulties connecting to the online help source.

- **Back and Forward buttons:** After browsing multiple helps topics in the search result window, you might want to navigate among results and various levels of detail. Click the Back or Forward button to perform your navigation.

 If you want to resize the help viewer window, move the mouse pointer to any edge of the window until the pointer changes to a double-headed arrow, and then drag the mouse.

Part 2

Managing Workbooks

Working with documents is critical to using any software. Microsoft Excel documents are known as *workbooks*. This part covers the procedures that you need to know to manage workbook documents efficiently.

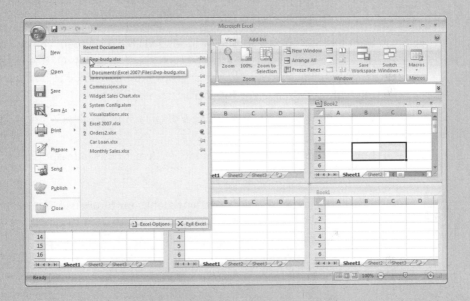

In this part . . .

- ✔ Arranging Windows Automatically
- ✔ Comparing Two Workbooks Side by Side
- ✔ Creating an Empty Workbook
- ✔ Creating Multiple Windows (Views) for a Workbook
- ✔ Opening and Saving Files
- ✔ Protecting and Unprotecting a Workbook
- ✔ Working with Workbook Templates

Activating a Workbook

A workbook is *active* when its window is maximized in the Excel window or after you select any part of the workbook when its window is not maximized. **See also** "Familiarizing Yourself with the Excel 2007 Window," in Part 1 and "Switching among Open Workbooks," later in this part.

Arranging Windows Automatically

If you want all your open workbook windows visible on-screen, you can move and resize them manually — or you can have Excel do it automatically. Follow these steps to make all open workbooks visible on the Excel screen:

1. Click the View tab in the Ribbon.

2. Click the Arrange All button. Excel displays the Arrange Windows dialog box.

3. Choose from the Tiled, Horizontal, Vertical, or Cascade options.

4. Click OK.

TIP

You can save the layout of your open workbooks for future use. **See** "Using a Workspace File," later in this part.

See also "Comparing Two Workbooks Side by Side," later in this part.

Changing the Default File Location

When you're opening a document in Excel, by default the Open dialog box points to the My Documents folder (Windows XP) or the Documents folder (Windows Vista) as the starting location to open documents. If you keep frequently used documents in a different folder, you may want the Open dialog box to point to this different folder to save some navigation steps. To change the default folder, follow these steps:

1. Click the Office button, and then click the Excel Options button. The Excel Options dialog box appears. The options are divided into sections, which appear in a list on the left side of the dialog box.

2. Click the Save section.

3. In the Default File Location text box, enter the path of the new default starting location to open documents. For example, if your new default document location is in a subfolder named Excel, which itself is in the My Documents or Documents folder, add \Excel to the default path. The new location in the text box should read C:\Users\Username\Documents\ Excel, where *Username* is the actual name of the user indicated in the text box.

4. Click OK.

Closing a Workbook

If you're no longer working with a workbook , you may want to close the workbook so that you can work on other documents without distraction. Closing unneeded workbooks also frees memory and minimizes potential screen clutter.

To close the unneeded workbook or workbooks, follow these steps:

1. If multiple workbooks are open, ensure that the workbook you want to close is active as follows: Click the View tab on the Ribbon, click the Switch Windows button, and select the workbook from the list of names in the menu.

2. Use any of the following methods to close the workbook:

   • Click the Office button and then choose Close.

   • Click the Close button on the far right of the Ribbon tab area (or on the workbook's title bar if the workbook is not maximized).

   • Double-click the Control button on the far left of the workbook's title bar if the workbook is not maximized.

   • Press Ctrl+F4.

   • Press Ctrl+W.

If you've made any changes to your workbook since the last time you saved it, Excel asks whether you want to save the changes before closing the workbook.

Comparing Two Workbooks Side by Side

Sometimes you have two versions of a workbook, and you want to compare the differences in the data visually. Excel provides a convenient feature that allows you to compare two documents side by side. To use this feature, follow these steps:

1. Open the workbooks you want to compare.

2. Click the View tab on the Ribbon and then click the View Side by Side button. Excel arranges the windows of the two workbooks horizontally. If you have more than two workbooks open, Excel displays a dialog box from which you select the name of the workbook you want to compare with the active workbook.

3. Click a worksheet tab in each workbook to display the worksheet data you want to compare.

4. In the View tab, click the Synchronous Scrolling button to toggle synchronized scrolling on and off. After you enable synchronized scrolling, the rows and columns in the two worksheets being compared scroll simultaneously.

5. You can click the Reset Window Position button in the View tab to ensure that the two workbook windows are sized equally and aligned horizontally. You need to use the button only if you adjust either or both window sizes during the current session.

TIP

You can save the layout of the open workbooks you're comparing for future use. **See** "Using a Workspace File," later in this part.

Creating an Empty Workbook

After you start Excel, it automatically creates a new (empty) workbook that it calls Book1. If you're starting a new project from scratch, you can use this blank workbook.

You can create another blank workbook in the following ways:

🗸 Press Ctrl+N.

🗸 Click the Office button, choose New, select Blank Workbook, and click Create.

You can add a button to the Quick Access toolbar that allows you to create a blank workbook with a single mouse click. Click the arrow to the right of the Quick Access toolbar and choose New from the menu. Excel adds the New button to the toolbar. **See also** "Working with the Quick Access Toolbar," in Part 1.

Creating Multiple Windows (Views) for a Workbook

Sometimes, you want to view two parts of a worksheet at once. Or you want to see more than one sheet in the same workbook at the same time. You can accomplish either of these actions by displaying your workbook in one or more additional windows.

To create a new view of the active workbook, click the View tab on the Ribbon and then click the New Window button. Excel displays a new window for the active workbook. To help you keep track of the windows, Excel appends a colon and a number to the workbook name in each window, as shown in Figure 2-1.

Figure 2-1

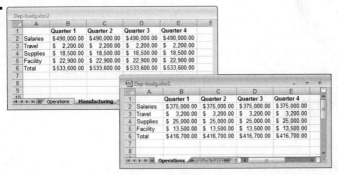

See also "Arranging Windows Automatically," earlier in this part, and "Comparing Two Workbooks Side by Side," earlier in this part.

Remember: A single workbook can have as many views (that is, separate windows) as you want.

Displaying multiple windows for a workbook also makes copying information from one worksheet to another easier. You can use Excel's drag-and-drop procedures to copy a cell, a range, or a chart. **See also** "Copying Cells and Ranges," in Part 4, and "Resizing, Moving, Copying, and Deleting an Embedded Chart," in Part 10.

Opening Nonstandard Files

In addition to files in its native format, Excel 2007 can open files in non-Excel 2007 formats, including older Excel and text files. Excel 2007 can open files that weren't saved in its native format by using filters to open the foreign file as a workbook document.

To open a file in a non-Excel 2007 format, follow these steps:

1. Click the Office button and then choose Open. Excel displays the Open dialog box.

2. Windows XP: In the Files of Type drop-down list, select the file type.

   Windows Vista: Click the button located above the Open and Close button and choose a file type from the menu. By default, the button text reads All Excel Files (*.xl*;*.xlsx;*.xlsm) but the text changes if you select a different file type.

3. Windows XP: In the Look In drop-down list, navigate to the folder that contains the file.

   Windows Vista: In the Folders window on the left side of the dialog box, navigate to the folder that contains the document. If the Folders window isn't displayed, click Folders.

4. Select the file and click Open, or double-click the filename.

See also "Opening a Workbook," immediately following this section.

Opening a Workbook

If you open a workbook in Excel, the entire document loads into memory, and any changes that you make occur only in the copy that's in memory.

To open an existing workbook , follow these steps:

1. Click the Office button and then choose Open to display the Open dialog box. Alternatively, press Ctrl+O or Ctrl+F12 to display the Open dialog box.

2. Windows XP: In the Look In drop-down list, navigate to the folder that contains the document.

   Windows Vista: In the Folders window on the left side of the dialog box, navigate to the folder that contains the document. If the Folders window isn't displayed, click Folder (see Figure 2-2).

3. Select the workbook in the selected folder and click Open, or double-click the filename.

 You can select more than one document in the Open dialog box. The trick is to press and hold Ctrl while you click each document. After you select all the documents you want, click Open.

Figure 2-2

Remember: You can open a workbook you have worked with recently without navigating through the Open dialog box. On the right side of the Office menu, Excel provides a Recent Documents list. If the document that you want to open appears in this list, you can choose it directly from the menu.

Protecting and Unprotecting a Workbook

Excel provides several levels of protection for your sensitive work. Here are some ways you can protect your workbooks. You can protect

- ✔ A workbook from being opened by unauthorized personnel

- ✔ A workbook from being saved with the same filename

- ✔ A workbook's structure (control the manipulation of worksheets in a workbook)

- ✔ A workbook's windows (control the sizing and positioning of a workbook's windows and any workbook views you create)

You should write down any passwords you use and store them in a safe location. If you forget or lose your passwords, you won't be able to undo the areas you protected by any normal means.

Safeguarding your workbook from unauthorized users

Follow these steps to restrict unauthorized personnel from opening or modifying a workbook:

1. Open a workbook or select an already opened workbook you want to protect.

2. Click the Office button and choose Save As. Excel displays the Save As dialog box.

3. Click Tools and choose General Options from the menu. Excel displays the General Options dialog box.

4. In the Password to Open text box, enter a password that must be used before a user can open the workbook.

5. In the Password to Modify text box, enter a password that must be used before a user can save the workbook under the same filename. Passwords can be up to 15 characters and are case sensitive.

6. Click OK. Excel asks you to reenter the passwords for confirmation.

7. Reenter the passwords.

8. Windows XP: In the Save In drop-down, select the folder in which to save the workbook and then click Save.

   Windows Vista: If the Folders window isn't displayed, click Browse Folders, click Folders to display the Folders window, and then select the folder in which to save the document. Then click Save.

9. If you're saving the workbook with the same name, respond when Excel displays a message asking you to confirm overwriting the file.

To remove passwords from the workbook, follow the previous steps, except delete the passwords in Step 4, Step 5, or both.

See also "Saving Files," later in this part.

 If you are using a workbook saved in an earlier version of Excel, Excel 2007 displays a message offering to convert the workbook to the Office XML file format (the default file format) before you save the workbook with passwords. You should choose to accept the suggestion only if you will not be sharing the workbook with users who have earlier versions of Excel. *See also* "Saving Files," later in this part.

The General Options dialog box offers other safeguarding options. Select the Always Create a Backup check box if you want Excel to always save a backup copy of the existing workbook before you save the workbook. If you select the Read Only Recommended check box, when the workbook is opened, Excel displays a message suggesting that the workbook be opened as read only. The user, however, can choose to ignore the suggestion.

Protecting and unprotecting a workbook structure or window

To protect a workbook structure or window properties from accidental or intentional alteration, follow these steps:

1. Click the Review tab on the Ribbon and then click the Protect Workbook button. Excel displays the Protect Workbook dialog box.

2. Select the appropriate check box(es), as follows:

   • *Structure* prevents any of the following changes to a workbook sheet: adding, deleting, moving, renaming, hiding, or unhiding.

   • *Windows* protects the workbook window from being moved or resized.

3. If you feel that you need a high level of protection, supply a password in the Password text box, and click OK. When Excel requests that you reenter the password for confirmation, do so.

4. Click OK.

To unprotect a workbook structure or window, click the Review tab on the Ribbon and then click the Unprotect Workbook button. If you did not supply a password when the workbook was protected, Excel unprotects the workbook automatically. Otherwise, Excel prompts you to enter a password.

Saving Files

When you save a workbook, Excel saves the copy in memory to your drive — overwriting the previous copy of the workbook. When you save a workbook for the first time, Excel displays its Save As dialog box.

Excel 2007 uses a new default format for saving workbook documents. This new format is based on the Extensible Markup Language (XML). Office 2007 applications use an extension to XML called Office Open XML. Workbooks saved in Office Open XML maintain full fidelity with everything in your document, including (in the case of Excel) formulas, formatting, charts, tables, and macros. XML and Office Open XML are text-based formats (versus the binary formats found in earlier versions of Office applications).

You don't need to have a complete (or even partial) knowledge of XML or Office XML to work in Excel 2007. However, it is useful to know that Excel 2007, like earlier versions, saves files with a different file extension depending on the type of file you are saving. A list of the standard file types and the extension names they use are given in the following table. We also include the corresponding file extensions used in earlier versions of Excel.

File Type	2007 Extension	Pre-2007 Extension
Excel workbook default format	.xlsx	.xls
Excel macro-enabled workbook	.xlsm	.xls
Excel workbook template	.xltx	.xlt
Excel macro-enabled workbook template	.xltm	.xlt
Excel binary workbook	.xlsb	.xls
Excel add-in	.xlam	.xla
Excel workspace	.xlw	.xlw
Excel user interface customization*	.xlb	.xlb

* In Excel 2007, you can customize the Quick Access toolbar as we discuss in Part 1. In earlier versions of Excel, you can customize an existing menu or toolbar or create a menu or toolbar. Excel saves these customizations automatically in an .xlb file, whose location depends on the operating system you're using (Windows XP or Windows Vista).

Remember: Unlike earlier versions of Excel, the table indicates that Excel 2007 workbooks or templates containing *macros* (scripts written to enhance Excel in some manner) are stored in files that differ from files without macros. If you attempt to save a macro-based workbook or template in a format that doesn't support macros (.xlsx or .xltx), Excel gives you the option to save the file without macros or to select a format that supports macros (.xlsm or .xltm).

Saving a workbook

Use any of the following methods to save the active workbook:

- ✔ Click the Office button and then choose Save.
- ✔ Click the Save button on the Quick Access toolbar.
- ✔ Press Ctrl+S.
- ✔ Press Shift+F12.

If the document you're saving does not yet have a name, Excel prompts you for a name by opening its Save As dialog box. You can give the document a name and navigate to the folder where you want to store the file. *See also* "Saving a workbook under a different name," in the next section.

Saving a workbook under a different name

Sometimes you may want to keep multiple versions of your work by saving each successive version under a different name.

To save a workbook with a different name, follow these steps:

1. Click the Office button and then choose Save As. Excel displays the Save As dialog box.

2. Windows XP: In the Save In drop-down list, select the folder in which to save the workbook.

   Windows Vista: If the Folders window isn't displayed, click Browse Folders, click Folders to display the Folders window, and then select the folder in which to save the workbook (see FIgure 2-3).

3. In the File Name text box, enter a new filename. (You don't need to include a file extension.)

4. Click Save.

Figure 2-3

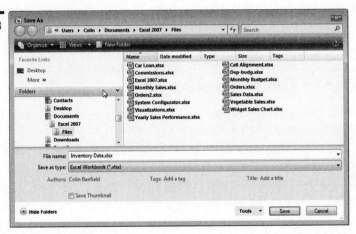

Excel creates a new copy of the workbook with a different name, but the original version of the workbook remains intact. (Note that the original workbook is no longer open.)

Saving a workbook in a different or earlier file format

To share a workbook with someone who uses an application that opens files in a format other than Excel 2007, be sure to save the workbook in a file format that the other application can read.

Excel can save workbook contents in many non-Excel file formats, such as, tab- or comma-delimited text, html, and standard xml.

To save a workbook in a different file format, follow these steps:

1. Click the Office button and then choose Save As.

2. In the Save As Type drop-down list, select the format in which you want to save the file. For example, to save in an earlier Excel file format, select Excel 97-2003 Workbook.

3. Click Save.

Excel separates a list of some Excel file formats from the complete list of file types to save you time in navigating the Save As dialog box. Click the arrow at the end of the Save As option in the Office menu to display the list of some common Excel file formats.

Remember: If you attempt to save a workbook with features not supported in the file format you're saving to, Excel displays a warning message. If the format you're saving to is an earlier version of Excel, Excel displays the Compatibility Checker dialog box, which shows you a list of features that will be lost.

Switching among Open Workbooks

If you have multiple workbooks open, the workbooks usually appear maximized on-screen so that you can view only one workbook at a time.

To switch the active display among workbooks, use one of the following methods:

✓ Click the View tab on the Ribbon, click the Switch Windows button, and then select one of the workbook names in the menu that appears.

✓ Press Ctrl+F6 or Ctrl+Tab to cycle the active display among the open workbooks.

Using a Workspace File

The term *workspace* refers to the layout of all the open workbooks — their screen positions and window sizes.

You may have a project that uses two or more workbooks, and you may like to arrange the windows in a certain way to make them easy to access at a later time. Fortunately, Excel enables you to save your entire workspace to a file. After you open the workspace file, Excel sets up the workbooks exactly as they were when you saved your workspace.

Opening a workspace file

To open a workspace file, follow the steps outlined for "Opening Nonstandard Files," earlier in this part, except in Step 2, select Workspaces (*.xlw) from the drop-down list (Windows XP) or menu (Windows Vista). Excel opens all the workbooks that you originally saved in the workspace.

See also "Saving a workspace file," the next section.

Saving a workspace file

To save your workspace, follow these steps:

1. Click the View tab on the Ribbon and then click the Save Workspace button. Excel displays the Save Workspace dialog box.

2. Use the filename that Excel proposes (for example, resume.xlw or resume), or enter a different name in the File Name text box.

3. Windows XP: In the Save In drop-down box, navigate to where you want to save the workspace.

    Windows Vista: If the Folders window isn't displayed, click Browse Folders, click Folders to display the Folders window, and then select the folder in which to save the workspace.

4. Click Save.

 A workspace file contains not the workbooks themselves but only the information that Excel needs to recreate the workspace. Excel saves the workbooks in standard workbook files. If you distribute a workspace file to a coworker, therefore, make sure that you also include the workbook files that the workspace file refers to.

Working with Workbook Templates

A *workbook template* is basically a workbook that contains one or more worksheets set up with formatting and formulas and ready for you to enter data and get immediate results. A workbook template can use any of Excel's features, such as charts, formulas, and macros. Excel includes templates that automate the common tasks of filling in invoices, expense statements, and purchase orders. You can also download several more templates from the Internet. You can also create your own templates from scratch or from an existing workbook.

Creating a workbook template

To save a workbook as a template, follow these steps:

1. Click the Office button and then choose Save As.

2. In the Save As Type drop-down list, select Excel Template.

3. If you want to save the template in a subfolder of the Templates folder in Windows XP: Excel displays the Templates folder in the Save In drop-down list. Select the subfolder in the Save In drop-down list.

   If you want to save the template in a subfolder of the Templates folder in Windows Vista: Click Browse Folders (if the Folders window isn't displayed) and click Folders to display the Folders window if necessary (the Templates folder is automatically selected after Step 2), and then select a subfolder.

   To create a new folder in the Templates folder in which you can save the template, click the Create New Folder button in the Save As dialog box and give the new folder a name.

4. In the File Name box, enter a name for the template, and then click Save. Excel saves templates with an .xltx file extension. If your template contains macros, Excel gives you the option to save the template without macros or to save in a format that supports macros (.xltm). *See also* "Saving Files," earlier in this part.

You can also save a template in an earlier file format. In Step 2, select Excel 97-2003 Template from the Save As Type drop-down list box.

To prevent overwriting the template file when you create a new workbook from a template, always save your templates in the Templates folder or a subfolder within the Templates folder.

Creating a workbook from a template

If you create a new workbook that you based on a template, Excel creates a copy of the template in memory so that the original template, on disk, remains intact. The default workbook name is the template name with a number appended to it. For example, if you create a new workbook based on a template by the name of Report.xltx, the workbook default name is Report1.xlsx. The first time that you save a workbook that you create from a template, Excel displays the Save As dialog box so that you can give the file a new name.

To create a workbook from a template, follow these steps:

1. Click the Office button and then choose New. Excel displays the New Workbook dialog box, as shown in Figure 2-4.

2. Select a template category from the list on the left side of the dialog box. The choices are as follows:

- **Blank and Recent:** This is the default category. From here you can select Recently Used Templates. Select a template and click Create to open a copy of the template file.

- **Installed Templates:** This category displays a gallery of templates installed in your system. Select a template and click Create to open a copy of the selected template.

- **My Templates:** This category contains templates you previously saved in the Templates folder or in a subfolder in the Templates folder. Click My Templates to display the New dialog box. Templates you create in the Templates folder appear in the My Templates tab. If you saved Templates in one or more subfolders in the Templates folder, the folder names appear as tabs in the New dialog box. Select a template from a tab and click OK. Excel opens a copy of the template.

- **New from Existing:** This category allows you to use any workbook as a template or to use a template file that's not in the Templates folder. Click New from Existing to display the New from Existing Workbook dialog box. Navigate to the folder containing the file you want to use as a template, select the file in the folder, and click Create New. Excel opens a copy of the file.

- **Microsoft Office Online:** If you are connected to the Internet, you can select from one of the online categories and Excel will display a list of available templates in the selected category. Choose a template, click Download, and Excel opens a copy of the template.

3. Save the workbook after you enter the appropriate data in the template copy. *See also* "Saving Workbooks" and "Creating a workbook template," earlier in this part.

Figure 2-4

Creating a default workbook template

You can create a default workbook template that defines the formatting or content of the new (blank) workbooks that open after you start Excel. Excel bases every new (blank) workbook that you open on the default workbook template. The default workbook template that you create replaces Excel's built-in default workbook template.

Follow these steps to create a default workbook template:

1. Create a new workbook. *See* "Creating an Empty Workbook," earlier in this part.

2. Add or delete as many worksheets as you want to appear in the new workbook. *See* "Adding a New Worksheet" and "Deleting a Worksheet," both in Part 3.

3. If you want, turn off the display of gridlines. See "Turning off Gridlines," in Part 3.

4. Apply the desired formatting, sheet names, text, styles, and so on. *See* Part 8 if you need help applying different formatting options.

5. Select a new theme for the template if you don't like Excel's default choice. *See* "Formatting with Themes," in Part 1.

6. Click the Office button, choose Save As, and select Excel Template from the Save As Type drop-down list.

7. Windows XP: In the Save In drop-down list, locate an xlstart folder. Excel can use more than one xlstart folder and will open all files located in these folders on startup. The xlstart folders normally reside in the following locations: C:\Documents and Settings*Username*\Application Data\Microsoft\Excel (where *Username* is your login username) and C:\Program Files\Microsoft Office\Office 12 folders, respectively.

   Windows Vista: If the Folders window isn't displayed, click Browse Folders, click Folders to display the Folders window, and then locate the xlstart folder. Excel can use more than one xlstart folder and will open all files located in these folders on startup. The xlstart folders normally reside in: C:\Users*Username*\AppData\Roaming\Microsoft\Excel (where *Username* is your login name) and C:\Program Files\Microsoft Office\Office 12 folders, respectively.

8. In the File Name text box, type **book.xlt**.

9. Click Save.

All new (blank) workbooks that you create are now replicas of the book.xlt workbook that you saved in Step 9.

You can always edit the book.xlt file or delete it if you no longer want to use it.

Part 3

Working with Worksheets

A workbook can consist of any number of *worksheets*. Each sheet has a tab that appears at the bottom of the workbook window. In this part, we discuss several useful things that you can do with worksheets.

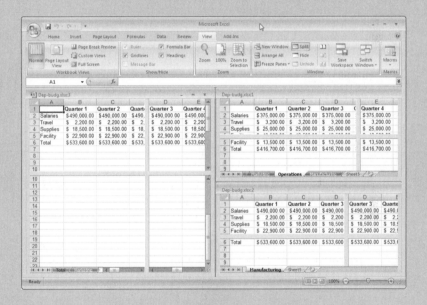

In this part . . .

- ✔ Adding and Deleting Worksheets
- ✔ Changing a Worksheet's Name
- ✔ Grouping and Ungrouping Worksheets
- ✔ Hiding and Unhiding a Worksheet
- ✔ Protecting a Worksheet
- ✔ Zooming a Worksheet

Activating a Worksheet

Before you can do any work in a worksheet, you must first activate it. To activate a worksheet, just click its tab. If the tab for the sheet that you want to activate isn't visible, use the tab scrolling buttons to scroll the sheet tabs. Figure 3-1 shows how Excel highlights the active sheet. You also can use the following shortcut keys to activate a different sheet:

   ✔ **Ctrl+PgUp:** Activates the previous sheet, if you have one.

   ✔ **Ctrl+PgDn:** Activates the next sheet, if you have one.

Figure 3-1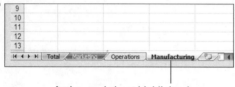

Active worksheet highlighted

Adding a New Worksheet

You can add a new worksheet to a workbook in the following ways:

   ✔ Click the Insert Worksheet tab button, which is located after the last worksheet tab in the workbook.

   ✔ Press Shift+F11.

In either case, Excel inserts a new worksheet and it becomes the active worksheet. The default name that Excel gives to the worksheet is the word *Sheet*, followed by a number.

Changing a Worksheet's Name

By default, Excel names its worksheets Sheet1, Sheet2, and so on. Providing more meaningful names helps you identify a particular sheet. To change a sheet's name:

   1. Double-click the sheet tab, or right-click the sheet tab and choose Rename from the menu that appears. Either method selects the text in the tab.

   2. Type the new sheet name directly on the tab.

Remember: Sheet names can be up to 31 characters long. Names can include spaces but not the following characters: [ ] (brackets); : (colon); / (slash); \ (backslash); ? (question mark); and * (asterisk).

Coloring a Worksheet Tab

Excel enables you to add color to a worksheet tab. You can use this feature, for example, to quickly identify a specific worksheet by its color. To color a worksheet tab, follow these steps:

1. Select the worksheet tab that you want to color.

2. Right-click the sheet tab, and choose Tab Color from the menu that appears.

3. Select a color for the tab from the color picker that appears.

To undo the tab color, follow the same procedure, but click the No Color option in the color picker.

Remember: If you select a tab that you have color-coded, the tab color appears below the sheet name. If a tab is fully colored, it's not currently selected.

Copying a Worksheet

You can copy a worksheet — and put the copy either in the original workbook or in a different workbook — in either of the following ways:

✔ Right-click the worksheet tab and choose Move or Copy from the menu that appears. Excel opens the Move or Copy dialog box, as shown in Figure 3-2. Select the location for the copy in the To Book drop-down list (to copy the sheet to a new or other open workbook) or the Before Sheet list box, or both. Make sure that the Create a Copy check box is selected. Click OK to make the copy.

✔ Click the worksheet tab, press Ctrl, and drag the sheet to the desired location in the workbook. As you drag, the mouse pointer changes to a small sheet with a plus sign on it, and a small arrow guides you. To use this method to copy a worksheet to another open workbook, you must first arrange the workbooks. *See* "Arranging Windows Automatically," in Part 2.

Remember: To copy a worksheet to a different workbook, both workbooks must be open.

Figure 3-2

If necessary, Excel changes the name of the copied sheet to make it unique within the workbook. If you copy a sheet by the name of Sheet1 to a workbook that already contains a Sheet1, for example, Excel changes the name of the copied sheet to Sheet1 (2). To change the name of a sheet, *see* "Changing a Worksheet's Name," earlier in this part.

Deleting a Worksheet

To delete a worksheet, right-click the sheet tab and choose Delete from the menu that appears. If the sheet you want to delete contains data (or if you delete all the data on a sheet in the current session), Excel asks you to confirm the fact that you want to delete the sheet. Every workbook must contain at least one sheet, so if you try to delete the only sheet, Excel complains.

 To select multiple sheets to delete, press Ctrl while clicking the sheet tabs that you want to delete. To select a group of contiguous sheets, click the first sheet tab, press Shift, and then click the last sheet tab.

 After you delete a worksheet, it's gone for good. This operation is one of the few in Excel that you can't undo. Therefore, you may want to save a workbook before deleting worksheets. Then, if you inadvertently delete a worksheet, you can revert to the saved version.

Freezing Row or Column Titles

Many worksheets are set up with row and column headings. As you scroll through such worksheets, you can easily get lost after the row and column headings scroll out of view. Excel provides a handy solution to alleviate this problem: freezing rows and columns.

To freeze entire rows or columns, follow these steps:

1. Move the cell pointer to the cell below the row that you want to freeze and to the right of the column that you want to freeze. Use the following steps to freeze various portions of the worksheet:

   • To freeze row 1 and column A, for example, move the cell pointer to cell B2.

   • To freeze rows only, move the cell pointer below the rows that you want to freeze in column A.

   • To freeze columns only, move the cell pointer to the right of the columns that you want to freeze in row 1.

2. Click the View tab on the Ribbon.

3. Click the Freeze Panes button and choose Freeze Panes from the menu. Excel inserts dark lines to indicate the frozen rows and columns. These frozen rows and columns remain visible as you scroll throughout the worksheet.

To unfreeze the frozen rows or columns, repeat Steps 2 and 3 but in Step 3, choose Unfreeze Panes from the menu. *See also* "Splitting Panes," later in this part.

You can quickly freeze the top row or left column by clicking the View tab on the Ribbon, clicking the Freeze Panes button, and choosing either Freeze Top Row or Freeze First Column from the menu. These options are useful because data is often stored in worksheets with labels in the top row, first column, or both. Note that the cell pointer can be in any location when you select either of these options.

An alternative to freezing row titles is to convert the range to a table. When table headers scroll off the sheet, Excel displays the header titles in the column header. *See* Part 11, "Working with Tables."

Grouping and Ungrouping Worksheets

Excel allows you to group multiple worksheets so that you can perform tasks on all the sheets in the group simultaneously. For example, you can group sheets to print, you can apply formatting to a given range in all the sheets in a group, or you can enter data into the same cell or range in all the sheets in the group. Any modifications you make to one sheet in the group are applied to the other sheets in the group.

Grouping worksheets

If the sheets you want to group are contiguous, follow these steps:

1. Select the tab of the first sheet by clicking it.

2. Press and hold down the Shift key and select the tab of the last sheet. Excel selects all the sheets between the first and last, inclusive.

If the sheets you want to group are not contiguous, follow these steps:

1. Select the tab of the first sheet by clicking it.

2. Press and hold down the Ctrl key and click the tabs of the other sheets in turn.

Remember: You can't switch among sheets in a group if all the sheets in the workbook are grouped. In this case, clicking any *inactive* sheet tab (any sheet tab with the name not highlighted) ungroups all the worksheets.

 If you need to group and switch among all your existing worksheets in the workbook, add a new (blank) worksheet first. *See also* "Adding a New Worksheet," earlier in this part.

Ungrouping worksheets

You can use any of the following methods to ungroup worksheets. The first three methods ungroup all worksheets; the last ungroups only an inactive sheet.

✔ Click any unselected sheet tab to ungroup all worksheets.

✔ Press and hold down the Shift key and click the *active* sheet tab (the sheet tab with the highlighted name) to ungroup all worksheets.

✔ If all the sheets in the workbook are grouped, click any *inactive* sheet tab to ungroup all worksheets.

✔ Press and hold down the Ctrl key and click an *inactive* sheet tab in the group to ungroup only that worksheet.

Hiding and Unhiding a Worksheet

Hiding a worksheet is useful if you don't want others to see it or if you just want to get it out of the way. If a sheet is hidden, its sheet tab is also hidden.

To hide a worksheet, right-click the worksheet tab and choose Hide from the contextual menu or click the View tab on the Ribbon and then click the Hide button. The selected worksheet is hidden from view.

You can select multiple sheets to hide at once. If the sheets you want to hide are contiguous, click the first sheet, press and hold down Shift, and click the last sheet. If the sheets are noncontiguous, click the first sheet, press and hold down Ctrl, and click the other sheets in succession.

Remember: Every workbook must have at least one visible sheet, so Excel doesn't allow you to hide all sheets in a workbook.

To unhide a hidden worksheet, follow these steps:

1. Right-click any visible sheet tab and click Unhide from the contextual menu, or click the View tab on the Ribbon and click the Unhide button. Excel displays the Unhide dialog box.

2. Select the sheet that you want to unhide, and click OK. You can unhide only one sheet at a time.

Moving a Worksheet

Sometimes, you may want to rearrange the order of worksheets in a workbook — or move a sheet to a different workbook.

First, select the sheet that you want to move by clicking the sheet tab. You can also move multiple sheets at once by pressing Ctrl while you click the sheet tabs that you want to move.

You can move a selected worksheet(s) in the following ways:

- ✔ Right-click the worksheet tab and choose Move or Copy from the contextual menu that appears. Excel opens the Move or Copy dialog box. Select the location for the move in the To Book drop-down list (to move the sheet to a new or other open workbook) or in the Before Sheet list box, or in both. Make sure that the Create a Copy check box is unchecked. Click OK to move the sheet.

- ✔ Click the sheet tab, and drag the sheet to its desired location in the workbook. As you drag, the mouse pointer changes to a small sheet, and a small arrow guides you. To use this method to move a worksheet to another open workbook, you must first arrange the workbooks. *See* "Copying a Worksheet," earlier in this part.

Remember: If you move a worksheet to a workbook that already contains a sheet by the same name, Excel changes the name to make it unique. For example, If you move Sheet1 to a workbook that already has a Sheet1, Excel changes the name of the sheet you are moving to Sheet1 (2). To change the name of a sheet, *see* "Changing a Worksheet's Name," earlier in this part.

Protecting a Worksheet

Deleting a single formula in a worksheet often creates a ripple effect, causing other formulas to produce an error value or, even worse, incorrect results. You can circumvent such problems by locking the cells that you don't want to be modified and then protecting your worksheets from modification by following these steps:

1. Right-click the tab of the worksheet you want to protect and choose Protect Sheet from the contextual menu, or click the Review tab on the Ribbon and click the Protect Sheet button. The Protect Sheet dialog box appears, as shown in Figure 3-3.

Figure 3-3

2. Provide a password in the Protect Sheet dialog box, if you want.

   • If you enter a password, you must reenter the password before the sheet can be unprotected.

   • If you don't supply a password, anyone can unprotect the sheet.

3. In the Allow All Users of This Worksheet To list box, click the appropriate check boxes to select the elements that users can change after the sheet is protected.

4. Click OK. If you entered a password in Step 2, Excel displays a dialog box for you to confirm the password.

Remember: By default, all cells or objects have their locked property turned on, which means that the cells or objects are locked when you protect the worksheet. Before protecting a worksheet, you normally want to unlock the input cells (the cells in which you enter data). To lock or unlock cells, first select them, and then right-click and choose Format Cells from the contextual menu; then check or uncheck the Lock check box on the Protection tab. ***See also*** "Selecting Cells and Ranges," in Part 4.

To remove protection from a protected sheet, right-click the worksheet you want to unprotect and choose Unprotect Sheet from the contextual menu, or click the Review tab on the Ribbon and click the Unprotect Sheet button. If the sheet was protected with a password, you have to enter the password before you can unprotect the sheet.

Publishing Your Worksheet Data to the Web

Web publishing is the process of placing your Excel data on a Web or intranet server as a Web page. In this process, you save your Excel data in HTML format so that users can view your data using an Internet browser. Excel provides several features designed to make the publishing process relatively painless.

To publish worksheet data to a Web page, follow these steps:

1. Select the worksheet containing the data you want to put on a Web page.

2. Click the Office button and then choose Save As. Excel displays the Save As dialog box.

3. In the Save As Type drop-down list, Select Web Page. Some new controls pertinent to Web publishing appear in the Save As dialog box, including the Publish button.

4. Click the Publish button.

5. In the Publish as Web Page dialog box that appears, make a selection from the Choose drop-down list. This list provides the following three main selections:

   • Previously published items: Use this option to republish data you've previously published.

   • Range of cells: Use this option to publish a range of cells in your worksheet. This option is automatically selected if you select the range prior to Step 2 of this procedure.

   • Items on *<Sheetname>*: Use this option to publish items in *<Sheetname>*, where *<Sheetname>* is the name of the worksheet in which you want to publish the items. This option is automatically selected if you don't select a specific item on *<Sheetname>* prior to Step 2 of this procedure.

   • Entire Workbook: Use this option to publish the entire workbook to a Web page.

6. In the list box below the Choose drop-down list, select the range or worksheet item that you want to publish.

If you select Items on *<Sheetname>* in Step 5, the selection box may display up to five items, depending on the objects in your worksheet. These items are Sheet (for example, all data), Chart, PivotTable, AutoFilter, and Print Area.

7. In the File Name text box, type the pathname and filename where you want to save your worksheet or worksheet items. Click the Browse button to help you locate the appropriate directory, folder, intranet, or Internet location.

   You may also check any or all of the following options:

   • Change: Click this button to add a title for the Web page.

   • File Name: Enter a name and location for your Web page if they are different from the name and location of your workbook file or use the Browse button to navigate to the file location.

   • Open Published Web Page in Browser: Select this check box to view the Web page in your browser after you save or publish it.

   • AutoRepublish Every Time This Workbook Is Saved: Select this check box if you want Excel to republish your workbook every time the workbook is saved. Using this option ensures that the data in your published location is always up to date.

8. Click the Publish button.

If you select the sheet, range, chart, PivotTable, AutoFilter, or print area prior to Step 2, you can skip the Publish as Web Page dialog box by clicking the Selection: *<Item>* radio button in the Save As dialog box. *<Item>* may be Sheet, Chart, PivotTable, AutoFilter, Print Area, or a range of cells. Most of the options in the Publish as Web Page dialog box are available, except Open Published Web Page in a Browser and AutoRepublish Every Time This Workbook Is Saved.

Remember: Excel embeds additional information that describes complex formatting options to the HTML file. Sometimes you can't view all the formatting options applied to your document if the file is open in a Web browser because many browsers can't interpret this additional information.

Splitting Panes

Splitting an Excel window into two or four panes enables you to view multiple parts of the same worksheet. Some of the key features of splitting panes are as follows:

✔ Clicking the View tab on the Ribbon and then clicking the Split button splits the active worksheet into two or four separate panes.

✔ The split occurs at the location of the cell pointer.

✔ You can use the mouse to drag and resize the pane.

✔ To remove the split panes, click the View tab on the Ribbon and then click the Split button.

A faster way to split and unsplit panes is to drag either the vertical or horizontal split bar, as shown in Figure 3-4. These split bars are standard elements of the Excel window and are located above and to the right of the vertical and horizontal scroll bars, respectively. To remove split panes by using the mouse, drag the pane separator all the way to the edge of the window or just double-click it.

Figure 3-4

	A	B	C	D	G	H	I	J	K	L
1	SalesPerson	OrderID	OrderDate	ShippedDate	ProductName	TotalPrice				
2	Buchanan, Steven	10248	7/4/1996	7/16/1996 0:00	Mozzarella di Giovanni	$174				
3	Buchanan, Steven	10248	7/4/1996	7/16/1996 0:00	Queso Cabrales	$168				
4	Buchanan, Steven	10248	7/4/1996	7/16/1996 0:00	Singaporean Hokkien Fri	$98				
5	Buchanan, Steven	10254	7/11/1996	7/23/1996 0:00	Guaraná Fantástica	$54				
6	Buchanan, Steven	10254	7/11/1996	7/23/1996 0:00	Pâté chinois	$403				
7	Buchanan, Steven	10254	7/11/1996	7/23/1996 0:00	Longlife Tofu	$168				
503	Davolio, Nancy	10567	6/12/1997	6/17/1997 0:00	Manjimup Dried Apples	$159				
504	Davolio, Nancy	10579	6/25/1997	7/4/1997 0:00	Rhönbräu Klosterbier	$163				
505	Davolio, Nancy	10579	6/25/1997	7/4/1997 0:00	Genen Shouyu	$155				
506	Davolio, Nancy	10587	7/2/1997	7/9/1997 0:00	Steeleye Stout	$360				
507	Davolio, Nancy	10587	7/2/1997	7/9/1997 0:00	Original Frankfurter grüi	$260				
508	Davolio, Nancy	10587	7/2/1997	7/9/1997 0:00	Gumbär Gummibärchen	$187				
509	Davolio, Nancy	10591	7/7/1997	7/16/1997 0:00	Aniseed Syrup	$140				
510	Davolio, Nancy	10591	7/7/1997	7/16/1997 0:00	Tourtière	$373				
511	Davolio, Nancy	10591	7/7/1997	7/16/1997 0:00	Uncle Bob's Organic Drie	$300				
512	Davolio, Nancy	10598	7/14/1997	7/18/1997 0:00	Schoggi Schokolade	$2,195				
513	Davolio, Nancy	10598	7/14/1997	7/18/1997 0:00	Fløtemysost	$194				
514	Davolio, Nancy	10604	7/18/1997	7/29/1997 0:00	Lakkalikööri	$180				

Sheet1 Sheet2 Sheet3 Shet

See also "Freezing Row or Column Titles," earlier in this part.

Turning Off Gridlines

Sometimes you're working with data to which you've applied a number of formatting options, but you find the worksheet gridlines distracting. In Excel 2007, turning the gridline display on and off is easy. Just click the View tab on the Ribbon and then click to clear the Gridlines check box.

Remember: Whether or not you have the gridline display turned on, gridlines aren't printed unless you select that option in the Sheet Options group of the Ribbon's Page Layout tab. **See also** "Printing gridlines or row and column headings," in Part 9.

Using Full-Screen View

If you want to see as much information as possible in a worksheet, Excel offers two options; you can hide the Ribbon controls or choose a full-screen view:

➤ **See** "Hiding the Ribbon commands from view," in Part 1.

➤ Click the View tab on the Ribbon and then click the Full Screen button. The Ribbon and its tabs, the Office button, the Quick Access toolbar, the formula bar, and the status bar all disappear. Press Esc to restore the hidden elements.

Zooming a Worksheet

Excel enables you to scale the size of your worksheets from 10 percent to 400 percent. Using a low zoom percentage can help you get a bird's-eye view of your worksheet to see its layout. A high zoom percentage can help you decipher very small text.

The easiest way to change the zoom factor of the active worksheet is to use the zoom control at the bottom right of the status bar (see Figure 3-5). You can drag the slider to zoom in and out or you can click the Zoom in (+) or Zoom out (–) buttons to change the view by 10 percent (per each click). The button on the immediate left of the Zoom out button displays the current zoom percentage. Clicking this button displays the Zoom dialog box. (You can open the Zoom dialog box also by clicking the View tab on the Ribbon and then clicking the Zoom button.)

Figure 3-5

 The Zoom dialog box is useful if you want to use a precise zoom level (by entering a value in the custom box) or zoom a selection — for example a range of cells or chart, to fit the worksheet window (by selecting the Fit Selection option).

 If you have a Microsoft IntelliMouse or equivalent device, you can zoom in or out in a worksheet by pressing Ctrl while you roll the mouse wheel.

Part 4

Entering and Editing Worksheet Data

This part deals with two of the most common tasks you're likely to perform on a daily basis in Excel: entering data into worksheet cells and editing (or changing) the data after you enter it. Excel provides many handy tools to make these tasks painless and efficient.

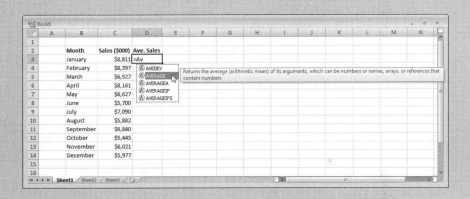

In this part . . .

- ✔ Copying Cells and Ranges
- ✔ Editing the Contents of a Cell
- ✔ Entering Dates, Formulas, Text, and Values
- ✔ Selecting Cells and Ranges
- ✔ Undoing Changes and Mistakes
- ✔ Validating Data Entry

Copying Cells and Ranges

Copying cells is a common spreadsheet operation, and several types of copying are possible. You can do any of the following:

- Copy one cell to another cell.
- Copy a cell to a range of cells. Excel copies the source cell to every cell in the destination range.
- Copy a range to another range.
- Copy multiple cells or ranges to another range.

Remember: Copying a cell normally copies the cell contents, its cell comment (if any), and the formatting that was applied to the original cell. If you copy a cell that contains a formula, the cell references in the copied formulas change automatically to relate to their new location.

Copying a cell to another cell or a range

To copy the contents of one cell to a range of cells, follow these steps:

1. Move the cell pointer to the cell that you want to copy (the source cell).

2. Click the Copy button in the Ribbon's Home tab. (You can also press Ctrl+C or right-click the cell and choose Copy from the contextual menu.)

3. Select the cell or range that you want to hold the copy (the destination cell or range).

4. Click the top part of the Paste split button in the Ribbon's Home tab. (You can also press Ctrl+V or right-click the destination cell or range and choose Paste from the contextual menu.)

   Excel displays the Paste Options Smart Tag next to the copied range. Clicking the Smart Tag provides a list of alternative paste options, as shown in Figure 4-1. For example, you can decide to match the destination formatting (otherwise, Excel copies the source data formatting by default) or copy formatting only (but not the data).

   If you don't need to use any of the options in the Paste Options Smart Tag, you can press Enter instead of clicking the Paste button.

5. Press Esc to complete the copy operation and remove the Paste Options Smart Tag. *Note:* This step isn't necessary if you press Enter in Step 4.

If the range you're copying to is adjacent to the cell you're copying from, you can drag the cell's AutoFill handle to copy the cell to the adjacent range. *See* "Filling a Series," later in this part.

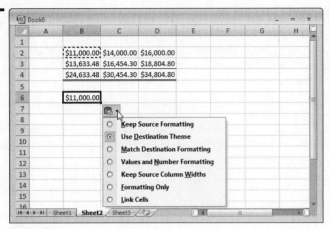

Figure 4-1

Copying a range to another range

To copy the contents of one range to another range of the same size, follow these steps:

1. Select the range that you want to copy.

2. Click the Copy button in the Ribbon's Home tab. (You can also press Ctrl+C or right-click the range and choose Copy from the contextual menu.)

3. Select the upper-left cell of the range that you want to use to hold the copy.

4. Click the top part of the Paste split button in the Ribbon's Home tab. (You can also press Ctrl+V or right-click the upper-left cell and choose Paste from the contextual menu.) If you don't need to use any of the options in the Paste Options Smart Tag, you can press Enter instead of using the Paste button.

5. Press Esc to clear the copy operation and remove the Paste Options Smart Tag. *Note:* This step isn't necessary if you press Enter in Step 4.

See also "Copying a cell to another cell or a range," earlier in this part.

If the location that you're copying to isn't too far away, you can follow these steps:

1. Select the cell or range to copy.

2. Press and hold Ctrl.

3. Move the mouse pointer to any of the selection's borders. The mouse pointer changes to an arrow with a small plus sign.

4. Drag the mouse to the location where you want to copy the cell or range. Excel displays an outline of the range as you drag with the mouse to help you see where you're going to paste the range.

5. Release the mouse button. Excel copies the cell or range to the new location.

Remember: If the mouse pointer doesn't change to an arrow in Step 3, your drag-and-drop feature is off. To turn on the drag-and-drop feature, follow these steps:

1. Click the Office button, and then click the Excel Options button. The Excel Options dialog box appears with a list of option sections in the left pane.

2. Click the Advanced section.

3. Select the Enable Fill Handle and Cell Drag-and-Drop check box.

4. To prevent accidental overwriting of data in the destination range, select the Alert before Overwriting Cells check box.

5. Click OK.

Copying data to another worksheet or workbook

To copy the contents of a cell or range to another worksheet or workbook, follow these steps:

1. Select the cell or range that you want to copy.

2. Click the Copy button in the Ribbon's Home tab. (You can also press Ctrl+C or right-click the cell or range and choose Copy from the contextual menu.)

3. Click the tab of the worksheet that you're copying to. If the worksheet is in a different workbook, activate that workbook (by clicking the View tab on the Ribbon, clicking the Switch Windows button, and selecting the workbook name from the menu) and then click the tab of the worksheet that will hold the copied data.

4. Select the upper-left cell of the range that will hold the copy.

5. Click the top part of the Paste split button in the Ribbon's Home tab. (You can also press Ctrl+V or right-click the destination cell or range and choose Paste from the contextual menu.)

6. Press Esc to complete the copy operation and remove the Paste Options Smart Tag.

See also "Copying a cell to another cell or a range" and "Copying a range to another range," both earlier in this part.

Copying multiple cells or ranges to another range

To copy noncontiguous cells or ranges to a single range elsewhere in the work-sheet, to a different worksheet in the same workbook, or to a range in a different workbook, you can copy and paste each cell or range in turn to the new range. However, Excel provides a simpler and less tedious method to perform this multiple-copy task. This method uses the *Office Clipboard* to copy multiple data items before pasting the items. The Office Clipboard differs from the *Windows Clipboard* in that the Windows Clipboard (which you use for copy-and-paste operations in most Windows applications) can store only one data item at a time.

The Office Clipboard can store 24 copied items. All Office applications share the Office Clipboard (and the 24-item limit), enabling you to cut and paste multiple items between Excel and other Office applications, such as Word and PowerPoint.

To copy multiple cells or ranges to another range, follow these steps:

1. Select the Home tab on the Ribbon if it isn't already selected and click the Clipboard group dialog launcher button, on the right of the group con-tainer. Excel displays the *Clipboard task pane,* as shown in Figure 4-2.

2. Select the first cell or range that you want to copy. (**See** "Selecting Cells and Ranges," later in this part.)

3. Click the Copy button in the Ribbon's Home tab. (You can also press Ctrl+C or right-click the cell or range and choose Copy from the contex-tual menu.) Excel copies the data to the Office Clipboard. The Clipboard task pane displays a portion of or all the copied data.

Figure 4-2

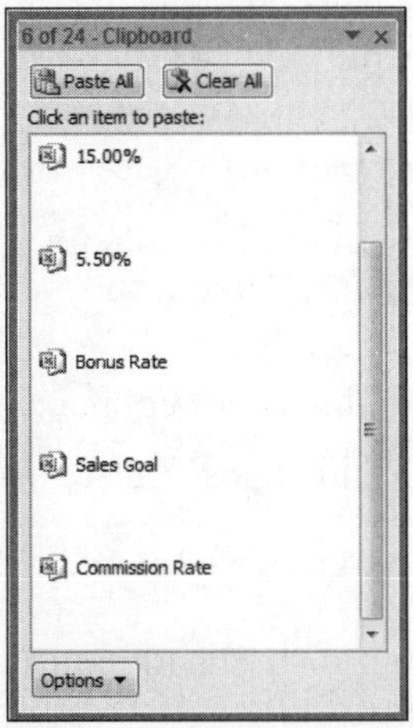

6 of 24 - Clipboard

Paste All   Clear All

Click an item to paste:

15.00%

5.50%

Bonus Rate

Sales Goal

Commission Rate

Options ▼

4. Select the next cell or range that you want to copy. (The cell or range can be from the same worksheet, another worksheet in the same workbook, or a worksheet in another open workbook.)

5. Repeat Steps 3 and 4 for all the remaining data that you want to copy.

6. Select the upper-left cell of the range that will hold the copied items.

7. Click the Paste All button in the Clipboard task pane. You can also click individual items in the Clipboard task pane to paste a single item at a time.

 You can enable the Office Clipboard by setting the Clipboard task pane to appear automatically after the second use of the Copy command. This option, if set, eliminates Steps 1 and 2. To turn on this option, click the Options button at the bottom of the Clipboard task pane and select the Show Office Clipboard Automatically option.

 Normally, you need to display the Clipboard task pane to enable the Office Clipboard. If you prefer to use the Office Clipboard without displaying the Clipboard task pane, click the Options button at the bottom of the Clipboard task pane and select the Collect Without Showing Office Clipboard option.

Remember: You can use the Office Clipboard for multiple cut operations in addition to the multiple copy operations that we discuss in this section.

Deleting Entire Rows and Columns

In certain circumstances, you may want to delete entire rows or columns from your worksheet. If you delete a row(s), the rows below the deleted row(s) shift upward to fill the gap. If you delete a column(s), the columns to the right of the deleted column(s) shift to the left to fill the gap.

To delete entire rows or columns, follow these steps:

1. Select the row header or column header of the row or column you want to delete. *See* "Selecting entire rows and columns," later in this part. Excel selects the entire row or column.

2. Use any of the following methods to delete the row or column:

   • Right-click the selected row or column and choose Delete from the contextual menu.

   • Press Ctrl+– (the minus sign).

   • Click the upper portion of the Delete button in the Ribbon's Home tab (the portion above the button's name).

Make sure that any cells that you want to keep aren't in the rows or columns you delete. You can zoom out in your worksheet to check for any cells that aren't normally visible on-screen. *See also* "Zooming a Worksheet," in Part 3.

Editing the Contents of a Cell

After you enter information into a cell, you can edit it. To edit the contents of a cell, use one of the following ways to get into cell-edit mode:

- ✔ Double-click the cell to edit the cell contents directly in the cell.
- ✔ Click the cell and press F2 to edit the cell contents directly in the cell.
- ✔ Click the cell that you want to edit; then click the formula bar to edit the cell contents in the formula bar.

All these methods cause the formula bar to display two new mouse icons. The following table describes these icons and what they do.

Icon	What It Does
✗	Cancels editing, and the cell's contents don't change. (Pressing Esc has the same effect.)
✓	Confirms the editing and enters the modified contents into the cell. (Pressing Enter has the same effect.)

Remember: If nothing happens after you double-click a cell, or if pressing F2 puts the cursor in the formula bar instead of directly in the cell, the in-cell editing feature is turned off. To turn on in-cell editing, follow these steps:

1. Click the Office button, and then click the Excel Options button. The Excel Options dialog box appears with a list of option sections in the left pane.

2. Click the Advanced section.

3. Select the Allow Editing Directly in the Cells check box.

4. Click OK.

If you're editing a cell that contains a formula, the name box (at the extreme left in the formula bar) displays a list of worksheet functions if you click the downward-pointing arrow next to the box. You can select a function from the list, and Excel provides assistance entering the arguments. The example in Figure 4-3 shows the contents of cell A1 after you double-click the cell for editing.

Figure 4-3

	SUM		▾	✕ ✓ *fₓ*	=A14*12	
	A	B	C	D	E	
1	=A14*12					
2						
3						
4						

If you're editing the contents of a cell (either directly in the cell or in the formula bar), the cursor changes to a vertical bar; you can move the vertical bar by using the direction keys. You can add new characters at the cursor's location. After you're in edit mode, you can use any of the following keys or key combinations to perform your edits:

- **Left arrow/right arrow:** Moves the cursor left or right one character, respectively, without deleting any characters.

- **Ctrl+left arrow/Ctrl+right arrow:** Moves the cursor one group of characters to the left or right, respectively.

- **Shift+left arrow/ Shift+right arrow:** Selects characters to the left or right of the cursor, respectively.

- **Shift+Home:** Selects from the cursor to the first character in the cell.

- **Shift+End:** Selects from the cursor to the last character in the cell.

- **Backspace:** Erases the character to the immediate left of the cursor.

- **Delete:** Erases the character to the right of the cursor or erases all selected characters.

- **Insert:** Places Excel in OVR (overtype) mode. Rather than adding characters to the cell, you *overtype,* or replace, existing characters with new ones, depending on the position of the cursor.

- **Home:** Moves the cursor to the beginning of the cell entry.

- **End:** Moves the cursor to the end of the cell entry.

- **Enter:** Accepts the edited data.

Remember: If you change your mind after editing a cell, you can click the Undo button on the Quick Access toolbar (or press Ctrl+Z) to restore the cell's previous contents.

You also can use the mouse to select characters while you're editing a cell. Just click and drag the mouse pointer over the characters that you want to select.

Remember: If the cell is locked and the worksheet is protected, you can't make any changes to the cell unless you unprotect the worksheet. **See** "Protecting a Worksheet," in Part 3.

Entering Data into a Range

Excel provides timesaving methods for you to enter data quickly in a range of cells. These methods are particularly helpful if you need to enter a lot of data manually.

Entering data into a specific range

If you're entering data into a range of cells, you may want to select the entire range of cells before you start entering data. This action causes Excel to move the cell pointer to the next cell in the selection after you press Enter.

The procedure works as follows:

- If the selection consists of multiple rows, Excel moves down the column; after it reaches the end of the column, it moves to the top of the next column.

- To skip a cell, press Enter without entering anything.

- To back up a row, press Shift+Enter. If you prefer to enter the data by rows rather than by columns, press Tab. To back up a column, press Shift+Tab.

Entering the same data into a range of cells

If you need to enter the same data (value, text, or formula) into multiple cells, your first inclination may be to enter it once and then copy it to the remaining cells. The following steps show you a better way:

1. Select all the cells that you want to contain the data. (*See* "Selecting a range," later in this part.)

2. Enter the value, text, or formula into the active cell in the range. This cell is already selected when you highlight the range.

3. Press Ctrl+Enter. Excel inserts the single entry into each cell in the selection.

Entering Dates and Times

Excel treats a date or a time as a value, but you format it to appear as a date or a time. If you work with dates and times, you need to understand Excel's date and time system.

Excel's system for working with dates uses a serial number system. The earliest date that Excel understands is January 1, 1900 (which has a serial number of 1). All other dates are counted from January 1, 1900. January 2, 1900 has a serial number of 2, January 1, 2007 has a serial number of 39083, and so on. Time is represented as a fraction of a day. For example, January 1, 2007 at 12:00:00 pm has a serial number of 39083.50. This system makes it easy to deal with dates and times in formulas.

Entering specific dates and times

Normally, you don't need to concern yourself with the Excel serial-number date system. You can simply enter a date in a familiar format, and Excel takes care of the details.

If you plan to use dates in formulas, make sure that the date you enter is one that Excel recognizes as a date (that is, a value); otherwise, your formula produces incorrect results. Excel is quite smart in recognizing dates that you enter into a cell, and it recognizes most common date formats. But it's not perfect. Excel interprets the following entries, for example, as text and not dates:

- ✔ June 1 2007

- ✔ Jun-1 2007

- ✔ Jun-1/2007

Remember: Excel uses a *windowing* approach for interpreting two-digit year entries. That is, within a 100-year window, Excel interprets 1/1/29 as January 1, 2029. If you enter 1/1/30, Excel interprets it as January 1, 1930. To be safe, enter the year as a four-digit value and then format it as you want.

The best way to deal with times is to enter the time into a cell in a recognized format. The following table lists some examples of time formats that Excel recognizes.

Entered into a Cell	*Excel's Internal Interpretation*
11:30:00 am	11:30 a.m.
11:30:00 AM	11:30 a.m.
11:30 pm	11:30 p.m.
11:30	11:30 a.m.

You also can combine dates and times, as follows.

Entered into a Cell	*Excel's Internal Interpretation*
January 1, 2007 12:00:00 pm	12:00 p.m. on January 1, 2007
6/1/07 11:30	11:30 a.m. on June 1, 2007

Entering the current date or time

If you need to date-stamp or time-stamp a cell in your worksheet, Excel provides the following two shortcut keys that perform this task for you:

- ✓ **Current date:** Press Ctrl+; (semicolon)

- ✓ **Current time:** Press Ctrl+Shift+; (semicolon)

Entering Formulas

A *formula* is a special type of cell entry that returns a result: After you enter a formula into a cell, the cell displays the result of the formula. The formula itself appears in the formula bar (which is just below the Ribbon) after you activate the cell.

A formula begins with an equal sign (=) and can consist of any of the following elements:

- ✓ Operators, such as + (for addition) and * (for multiplication)

- ✓ Cell references, including addresses such as B4 or C12, as well as named cells and ranges

- ✓ Values and text

- ✓ Worksheet functions (such as SUM)

You can enter a formula into a cell in one of two ways: manually (by typing it in) or by pointing to cell references. ***See also*** "Basic Formula Essentials," in Part 5, for more information on operators and operator precedence.

Entering formulas manually

To enter a formula manually, follow these steps:

1. Move the cell pointer (by clicking the cell with the mouse pointer or navigating with the arrow keys) to the cell that you want to hold the formula.

2. Type an equal sign (=) to signal the fact that the cell contains a formula.

3. Type the formula and press Enter.

As you type, a drop-down list appears below the cell. This is Excel's new Formula AutoComplete feature. The feature tries to anticipate what you're typing and presents a list of matched items, as shown in Figure 4-4.

Figure 4-4

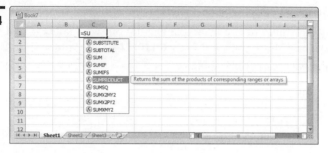

To select an item from the list, simply double-click the item or press the Tab key and Excel inserts the item in the formula.

Here are some of the types of items that appear in the Formula AutoComplete drop-down list:

- Excel built-in functions: All functions in the Excel library. **See also** "Entering functions manually," in Part 5.

- User-defined functions: Custom functions that supplement Excel's built-in functions through add-ins or through functions defined in the workbook (using Excel's macro language.) **See also** "Using Add-In Functions," in Part 5.

- Defined names: All names you define in the workbook. **See also** Part 6, "Creating and Using Names."

You will notice that the characters you type appear in the cell as well as in the formula bar. When entering a formula, you can use all the normal editing keys (Delete, Backspace, direction keys, and so on).

As you enter a formula, Excel shows each cell reference in the formula in a different color. If the reference cells are visible on the worksheet, you see a border around each cell in the same color as the cell reference in the formula. This feature makes it easier to identify the references of the cells you're typing in your formulas.

See also "Entering formulas by pointing," immediately following in this section.

TIP

If you find the Formula AutoComplete feature distracting, or you simply want to disable it temporarily, follow these steps to turn off the feature:

1. Click the Office button, and then click the Excel Options button. Excel displays the Excel Options dialog box with a list of option sections in the left pane.

2. Click the Formulas section.

3. Click to clear the Formula AutoComplete check box.

4. Click OK.

Entering formulas by pointing

The pointing method of entering a formula still involves some manual typing. The advantage is that you don't need to type the cell or range references. Instead, you point to them in the worksheet, which is usually more accurate and less tedious.

The best way to explain this procedure is with an example. Follow these steps to enter the formula =**A1/A2** into cell A3 by using the pointing method:

1. In cell A1, type **12000** and press Enter.

2. Move the cell pointer to cell A3 (by clicking the cell or navigating with the arrow keys). This cell is where you want the formula (and the result) to go.

3. Type an equal sign (=) to begin the formula.

4. Press the up-arrow key twice. As you press this key, notice that Excel displays a moving border around the reference cell (A1) and the cell reference appears in cell A3 and in the formula bar (see Figure 4-5).

   Excel colors the cell reference in the formula and the moving border around the reference cell (A1) with the same color.

5. Type a division sign (/). Excel now displays a solid-colored border around the A1 cell reference.

6. Press the up-arrow key once. Excel adds A2 to the formula. Excel now displays a different color for the new cell reference in the formula and the same color for the border of the new reference cell.

7. Press Enter to end the formula entry.

See also "Entering formulas manually," earlier in this part.

Figure 4-5

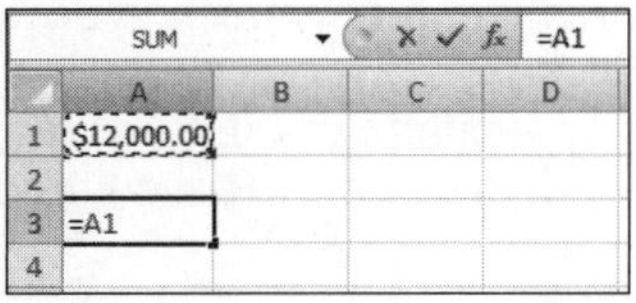

Entering Text

You can use text in worksheets to serve as labels for values and headings for columns, or to provide instructions about the worksheet. An entry of mixed text and numbers is still considered text. A cell can hold as many as 32,767 characters.

Entering text into cells

To enter text (rather than a value or a formula) into a cell, follow these steps:

1. Move the cell pointer to the appropriate cell (by clicking the cell with the mouse pointer or by navigating with the arrow keys).

2. Type the text.

3. Press Enter or any of the direction keys.

If you enter text that's longer than the column's current width, one of the following happens:

✔ If the cells to the immediate right are blank, Excel displays the text in its entirety, spilling the entry into adjacent cells.

✔ If an adjacent cell isn't blank, Excel displays as much of the text as possible. (The cell contains the full text; it just doesn't display all of it.)

In either case, you can always see the text (as you type it and after you type it) because it appears in the formula bar as well as in the cell. In previous versions of Excel, if you had text or a formula in a cell that exceeded the character width of the formula bar, the formula bar would spill into the sheet to display the contents of the cell, often obscuring column headers and sheet content.

In Excel 2007, the formula bar has its own space that never overlaps with the worksheet grid. By default, the formula bar displays a cell's contents on one line. If the length of the cell contents exceeds the display capacity of a single line on the formula bar, Excel adds scroll arrows on the formula bar, as shown in Figure 4-6. You can view multiple lines of a cell's content on the formula bar (one line at a time) by clicking the up or down scroll arrows. If you want to keep multiple lines of a cell's content in view on the formula bar, you can adjust the height of the formula bar by dragging the resize bar at the bottom of the formula bar. As you drag the resize bar downwards, the worksheet grid is pushed down to accommodate the expanded formula bar. Clicking the Auto expand/collapse button at the far right of the formula bar (or pressing Ctrl+Shift+U) toggles between a single-line display and an expanded-line display (based on the last drag setting.)

Figure 4-6

| | SUM | ▾ (X ✓ fx | =H140*ROUND(IFERROR(VLOOKUP(mpn,ancillary_price_table,5,FALSE),0),0)*IF(Currency_Symbol="$ US",1,(1/ |
| | | | Exchange_Rate)) |

▲	A	C	D	E	F	G	H	I	J	K	L	M	N	O	P	Q	R	S	T
137		GX5000 cabinet isolation plates(1)					2				110		64						
138		Nylon isolation bushing					6				36		21						
139		Hex cap screw, 12mm x 120mm					4												
140		Isolation standoff					2				=H140*ROUND(IFERROR(VLOOKUP(mpn,ancillary_price_table,5,FALSE),0),0)*IF(Currency_Symbol="$ US",1,(								
141		Threaded rod - 1/2" x 6"					2				1/Exchange_Rate))								
142		Nuts 3014-7 - 1/2" (1)					6												

Remember: To display a long text entry that's adjacent to a cell that contains an entry, you can edit your text to make it shorter, increase the width of the column, or wrap the text within the cell so that it occupies more than one line. *See also* "Modifying Cell Size," in Part 8.

Completing text entries by using AutoComplete

If you're entering a lot of repeated text entries into a column, AutoComplete can help you speed up the process. AutoComplete enables you to type the first few letters of a text entry into a cell, and Excel automatically completes the entry based on other entries you've already made in the column. Your column entries must be contiguous (that is, have no blank cells between entries). AutoComplete doesn't work with entries in a row.

AutoComplete works with no effort on your part; just follow these steps:

1. Begin entering text or a value. If Excel recognizes your entry, it automatically completes it.

2. If Excel guesses correctly, press Enter to accept it. To enter something else instead, just continue typing and ignore Excel's guess.

 You can access this feature also by right-clicking the cell and choosing Pick from Drop-down List. If you use this method, Excel displays a list of all the entries in the current column. Just click the one you want, and Excel enters it automatically.

Remember: AutoComplete works only with pure text or mixed text (text and values); it doesn't work with pure values.

Entering Values

Values, also known as numbers, represent a quantity of some type: revenue, number of units, test scores, and so on. Values can stand on their own, or you can use the values you enter into cells as part of a formula or in creating a chart. Excel's numbers are precise up to 15 significant digits. If you enter a larger number, Excel stores it with only 15 digits of precision.

Entering values into cells

To enter a numeric value into a cell, follow these steps:

1. Move the cell pointer to the appropriate cell (by clicking the mouse pointer in the cell or by navigating with the arrow keys).

2. Enter the value.

3. Press Enter, Tab, or any of the direction keys. The value is displayed in the cell and also appears in the formula bar.

You can also include a decimal point, dollar sign, plus sign, minus sign, and comma. If you precede a value with a minus sign or enclose it in parentheses, Excel considers the value a negative number.

Remember: Sometimes the value doesn't appear exactly as you enter it. Excel may convert very large numbers to scientific notation. The formula bar, however, always displays the value that you originally entered.

Entering fractions

To enter a fraction into a cell, leave a space between the whole number part and the fractional part. To enter the decimal equivalent of 6⅞, for example, follow these steps:

1. Type **6**.

2. Type a space.

3. Type **7/8**.

4. Press Enter. Excel enters 6.875 into the cell and automatically formats the cell as a fraction. *See also* "Formatting a Number," in Part 8.

If the value has no whole number part (for example, ⅛), you must enter a zero and a space first, as follows: **0 1/8** — otherwise, Excel interprets the entry as January 8 of the current year.

Erasing Data in Cells and Ranges

To erase the contents of a cell but leave the cell's formatting and cell comments intact, perform the following two steps:

1. Select the cell or range that you want to erase. (*See* "Selecting Cells and Ranges," later in this part, for details.)

2. Press Delete.

 For more control over what you delete, click the Clear button in the Ribbon's Home tab and select an option from the menu. The menu contains the following four choices:

- ✔ **All:** Clears everything from the cell.

- ✔ **Formats:** Clears only the formatting and leaves the value, text, or formula.

- ✔ **Contents:** Clears only the cell's contents and leaves the formatting.

- ✔ **Comments:** Clears the comment attached to the cell (if a comment exists).

Filling a Series

Excel provides an AutoFill feature, which enables you to fill in several types of data series in a row or column. AutoFill uses the fill handle — the small square that appears at the bottom-right corner of the selected cell or range.

Excel provides an AutoFill Options Smart Tag next to the fill handle after you drag the fill handle to a new location. Click the AutoFill Options Smart Tag to display a list of commonly used fill options, such as Copy Cells, Fill Series, Fill Formatting Only, and Fill Without Formatting (see Figure 4-7).

Figure 4-7

Remember: If the selected cell or range doesn't have a fill handle, it means the AutoFill feature is turned off. To turn on the feature, follow these steps:

1. Click the Office button, and then click the Excel Options button. Excel displays the Excel Options dialog box with a list of option sections in the left pane.

2. Click the Advanced section.

3. Select the Enable Fill Handle and Cell Drag-and-Drop check box.

4. Click OK.

Remember: You can't use AutoFill if you make a multiple selection.

Entering a series of incremental values or dates

To use AutoFill to enter a series of incremental values, follow these steps:

1. Enter at least two values or dates in the series into adjacent cells. These values need not be consecutive.

2. Select the cells that you used in Step 1. (**See** "Selecting a range," later in this part, for details.)

3. Click and drag the fill handle to complete the series in the cells that you select. As you drag the fill handle, Excel displays a small box that tells you what it's planning to enter into each cell.

Remember: After you complete the drag operation, Excel displays the Auto Fill Options Smart Tag. You can click the Smart Tag to select a different fill option. For even more control, drag the fill handle while pressing the right mouse button. After you release the button, you see a list of options.

AutoFill also works in the negative direction. If you use AutoFill by starting with two cells that contain –20 and –19, for example, Excel fills in –18, –17, and so on.

If the values in the cells that you enter don't have equal increments, Excel completes the series by calculating a simple linear regression. This feature is handy for performing simple forecasts. **Note:** Excel calculates a simple linear regression or progression, depending on the direction (negative or positive) of the series.

Entering a series of text

Excel is familiar with some text series (days of the week, months of the year), and it can complete these series for you automatically.

Follow these steps to use AutoFill to complete a known series of text:

1. Enter any of the series into a cell (for example, **Monday** or **February**).

2. Click and drag the fill handle to complete the series in the cells that you select.

You can also teach Excel to recognize custom series that work with AutoFill. **See** "Sorting based on a custom sort order," in Part 11.

Inserting Entire Rows and Columns

If you insert new rows or columns in Excel, the program places blank rows or columns in the worksheet, and surrounding rows or columns move out to accommodate the new rows or columns.

To insert new rows or columns in your worksheet, follow these steps:

In certain circumstances, you may want to delete entire rows or columns from your worksheet. If you delete a row(s), the rows below the deleted row(s) shift upward to fill the gap. If you delete a column(s), the columns to the right of the deleted column(s) shift to the left to fill the gap.

To delete entire rows or columns, follow these steps:

1. Select the row header or column header of the row or column you want to delete. *See also* "Selecting entire rows and columns," later in this part. Excel selects the entire row or column.

2. Use any of the following methods to insert the row or column:

   - Right-click the selected row or column and choose Insert from the contextual menu.

   - Press Ctrl+Shift++ (the plus sign on the top row of keys) or Ctrl++ (the plus sign on the numeric keypad).

   - Click the upper or left portion of the Insert split button in the Ribbon's Home tab (at lower screen resolutions, the button is smaller and you click the left side).

Moving Cells and Ranges

Moving the data in a cell or a range is common. You may, for example, need to relocate a range of data to make room for something else.

Moving data to a new location in the same worksheet

Follow these steps to move a cell or range:

1. Select the cell or range to move. (*See* "Selecting Cells and Ranges," later in this part, for details.)

2. Click the Cut button in the Ribbon's Home tab. (You can also press Ctrl+X or right-click the cell or range and choose Cut from the contextual menu.)

3. Move the cell pointer to the range that will hold the copy (by clicking the cell or by navigating with the arrow keys). You need to select only the upper-left cell in the range.

4. Press Enter.

If the range that you're moving contains formulas that refer to other cells, the references continue to refer to the original cells. You almost always want references to continue to refer to the original cells.

If the location that you're moving to isn't too far away, you can follow these steps:

1. Select the cell or range to move. (*See* "Selecting Cells and Ranges," later in this part.)

2. Move the mouse pointer to any of the selection's borders. The mouse pointer changes to an arrow with a small directional cross at its tip.

3. Drag the mouse to the location where you want to move the cell or range.

   4. Release the mouse button. Excel moves the cell or range to the new location.

 If you press and hold Shift while dragging, Excel performs a move and an insert paste in a single operation, without use of the Insert dialog box. The Insert paste operation allows you to insert the cell or range inside another range.

 Remember: If you change your mind after Step 2, press Esc to cancel the operation. If you change your mind after you move the data, you can click the Undo button on the Quick Access Toolbar or press Ctrl+Z.

Remember: If the mouse pointer doesn't change to an arrow in Step 2, your drag-and-drop feature is off. To turn on the drag-and-drop feature, follow these steps:

   1. Click the Office button, and then click the Excel Options button. The Excel Options dialog box appears with a list of option sections in the left pane.

   2. Click the Advanced section.

   3. Select the Enable Fill Handle and Cell Drag-and-Drop check box.

   4. To prevent accidental overwriting of data in destination range, select the Alert before Overwriting Cells check box.

   5. Click OK.

 If you move data, make sure that you have enough blank cells to hold it. Excel overwrites existing data without warning.

Moving data to a different worksheet or workbook

If you want to move the contents of a cell or range to a different worksheet or to a different workbook, follow these steps:

   1. Select the cell or range to move. (***See*** "Selecting Cells and Ranges," later in this part, for details.)

 2. Click the Cut button in the Ribbon's Home tab. (You can also press Ctrl+X or right-click the cell or range and choose Cut from the contextual menu.)

   3. Activate the worksheet you're moving to by clicking the sheet tab. If you're moving the selection to a sheet on a different workbook, activate that workbook first by clicking the Switch Windows button on the Ribbon's View tab and selecting the workbook from the menu. (You can select a different workbook also by selecting the workbook name on the Windows taskbar below the Excel window.) After you activate the workbook, select the destination worksheet for the data.

   4. Move the cell pointer to the range that will hold the copy (by clicking the cell or by navigating with the arrow keys). You only need to select the upper-left cell in the range.

   5. Press Enter.

After you move data, make sure that you have enough blank cells to hold it. Excel overwrites existing data without warning.

Remember: If you change your mind after Step 2, press Esc to cancel the operation. If you change your mind after you move the data, you can click the Undo button on the Quick Access Toolbar or press Ctrl+Z.

Replacing the Contents of a Cell

To replace the contents of a cell with something else, follow these steps:

1. Select the cell. (***See*** "Selecting a cell," later in this part, for details.)

2. Type your new entry. (It replaces the previous contents.)

Remember: Any formatting that you applied to the cell remains.

Searching for Data to Replace

Sometimes you may need to replace all occurrences of a value or text with something else. If your worksheet contains lots of data, you may find locating a particular piece of information difficult. A quick way to find something is to have Excel do it for you.

To replace all occurrences of a value or text with something else:

1. Click the Find & Select button in the Ribbon's Home tab and choose Replace from the menu. (Alternatively, press Ctrl+H.) Excel displays its Find and Replace dialog box with the Replace tab selected, as shown in Figure 4-8.

2. In the Find What drop-down list, enter the text or value to search for.

3. If you want to search for data with specific formatting:

   a. Click the Format button to the right of the Find What drop-down list. If the Format button isn't visible, click the Options button. Excel displays the Find Format dialog box.

   b. Select the appropriate tabs, and in each tab, specify the formatting that you're looking for.

   c. After you complete your selections, click OK to exit the Find Format dialog box.

Figure 4-8

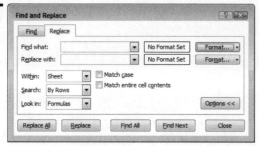

If a cell in your worksheet already contains all the formatting you want to use in your search, click the arrow on the Format button to the right of the Find What drop-down list and select Choose Format From Cell. Excel adds an eyedropper icon to the cursor. Click the cell that has the formatting you require.

4. In the Replace With drop-down list, enter the text or value that should replace the text or value from Step 2.

5. If you want to specify new formatting for the replaced characters, click the Format button to the right of the Replace With drop-down list box and follow the procedure outlined in Step 3.

6. In the Within drop-down list box, select whether you want to look in the active sheet or the entire workbook for the information that you typed in Step 2. If the Within drop-down box isn't visible, click the Options button.

7. To have Excel search and replace all occurrences automatically, click the Replace All button. To verify each replacement instead, click the Find Next button. Excel pauses after it finds a match. To replace the found text, click Replace. To skip it and find the next match, click the Find Next button again. Click the Find All button to select a match from the drop-down window.

8. Click the Close button after you finish finding and replacing the text.

See also "Finding Specific Data," in Part 7.

Selecting Cells and Ranges

In Excel, you normally select a cell or range before performing an operation that works with the cell or range. Topics in this section describe how to make various types of cell and range selections.

Selecting a cell

To select a cell (and make it the active cell), use any of the following techniques:

- ✔ Use the arrow keys to move the cell pointer to the cell.

- ✔ Click the cell with the mouse pointer.

- ✔ Click the Find & Select button in the Ribbon's Home tab and choose Go To from the menu (or press F5 or Ctrl+G), enter the cell address in the Reference text box of the Go To dialog box that appears, and click OK.

The selected cell now has a dark border around it, and its address appears in the name box.

Selecting a range

You can select a range in any of the following ways:

- ✔ Click the mouse in a cell and drag to highlight the range. If you drag past the end of the screen, the worksheet scrolls.

- ✔ Move to the first cell of the range. Press F8, and then move the cell pointer with the direction keys to highlight the range. Press F8 again to return the arrow keys to normal movement.

- ✔ Press Shift as you use the arrow keys to select a range.

- ✔ Click the Find & Select button in the Ribbon's Home tab and choose Go To from the menu (or press F5 or Ctrl+G), enter a range's address in the Reference text box of the Go To dialog box that appears, and click OK.

Selecting noncontiguous ranges

Most of the time, the ranges that you select are *contiguous* — they are a single rectangle of cells. Excel also enables you to work with noncontiguous ranges, which consist of two or more ranges (or single cells) that aren't necessarily next to each other (also known as a *multiple selection*).

To apply the same formatting to cells in different areas of your worksheet, for example, one approach is to make a multiple selection. After you select the appropriate cells or ranges, Excel applies the formatting that you choose to all the selected cells. Figure 4-9 shows two noncontiguous ranges (B2:F2 and B6:F6) that have been selected.

You can select a noncontiguous range in any of the following ways:

- ✔ Drag the mouse to select the first range, then press and hold Ctrl as you drag the mouse to select the other ranges.

Figure 4-9

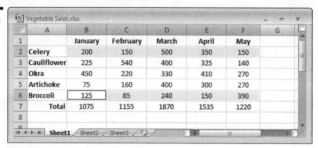

✔ From the keyboard, select the first range by pressing F8 and then using the arrow keys. After selecting the first range, press Shift+F8, move the cell pointer using the arrow keys, and press F8 to start selecting another range.

✔ Click the Find & Select button in the Ribbon's Home tab, choose Go To from the menu (or press F5 or Ctrl+G), and enter a range's address in the Reference text box of the Go To dialog box that appears. Separate the different ranges with a comma. Click OK, and Excel selects the cells in the ranges that you specify.

Selecting entire rows and columns

You can select entire rows or columns in any of the following ways:

✔ Click the row or column heading to select a single row or column.

✔ To select multiple adjacent rows or columns, click a row or column heading and drag to highlight additional rows or columns.

✔ To select multiple (nonadjacent) rows or columns, press Ctrl as you click the row or column headings that you want.

✔ Press Ctrl+spacebar to select the column of the active cell or the columns of the selected range.

✔ Press Shift+spacebar to select the row of the active cell or the rows of the selected cells.

✔ Either click the Select All button at the intersection of the row and column headers or press Ctrl+A or press Ctrl+Shift+spacebar to select all rows. Selecting all rows is the same as selecting all columns, which is the same as selecting all cells.

Selecting a multisheet (3-D) range

An Excel workbook can contain more than one worksheet, and a range can extend across multiple worksheets. You can think of these as three-dimensional ranges.

To select a multisheet range, follow these steps:

1. Select a cell or range on the active sheet. **See** "Selecting a range," earlier in this part.

2. Group the sheets that will be in the range. **See** "Grouping and Ungrouping Worksheets," in Part 3.

After you select a multisheet range, you can perform the same operations that you can perform on a single sheet range. Any changes you make to one sheet (formatting, entering or editing data, and so on) are reflected in the other sheets.

Transposing a Range

If you need to change the orientation of a range, Excel can do it for you in a snap. If you transpose a range, rows become columns and columns become rows. Figure 4-10 shows an example of a horizontal range that we transposed to a vertical range.

Figure 4-10

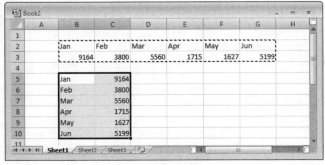

To transpose a range, follow these steps:

1. Select the range to transpose. (**See** "Selecting a range," earlier in this part, for details.)

2. Click the Copy button in the Ribbon's Home tab. (You can also press Ctrl+C or right-click the cell or range and choose Copy from the contextual menu.)

3. Click the upper-left cell where you want the transposed range to go. The transposed range can't overlap the original range.

4. Click the bottom half of the Paste split button (the part with the downward arrow) in the Ribbon's Home tab and choose Transpose from the menu.

5. Delete the original range, if necessary.

Remember: Excel adjusts any formulas in the original range so that they work correctly after you transpose them.

Undoing Changes and Mistakes

One very useful feature in Excel is its multilevel Undo feature. This feature means that you can reverse your recent actions, one step at a time. If you discover that you accidentally deleted a range of data several minutes ago, for example, you can use the Undo feature to backtrack through your actions until the deleted range reappears.

To undo an operation, use any of the following techniques:

 ✔ Click the Undo button on the Quick Access toolbar until you arrive at the action that you want to undo.

 ✔ Press Ctrl+Z until you arrive at the action that you want to undo.

 ✔ Click the arrow on the Undo button on the Quick Access toolbar. This action displays a description of your recent actions. Select the actions that you want to undo.

In Excel 2007 you can undo a maximum of 100 operations. In earlier versions of Excel, you can undo a maximum of 16 operations.

Validating Data Entry

You can specify the type of data that a cell can accept. If you develop a spreadsheet that others use, for example, you can limit the range of values that a user may enter into input cells. Excel then validates the input to ensure that the values the user enters fall within the range you specified. Excel displays an error message if a user enters an invalid value.

To specify data-entry validation criteria, follow these steps:

1. Select the cell or range that you want to validate. (*See* "Selecting Cells and Ranges," earlier in this part, for details.)

2. Click the Data tab on the Ribbon and click the upper portion of Data Validation split button (the portion above the button label) or click the lower portion of the button and choose Data Validation from the menu. Excel displays the Data Validation dialog box.

3. Click the Settings tab, and specify the type of data that the cell should have by selecting an entry from the Allow drop-down list box and the Data drop-down list box, if applicable.

To limit the entry in a cell to whole numbers between 100 and 200, for example, select Whole Number in the Allow drop-down list box, select Between in the Data drop-down box, enter **100** in the Minimum text box, and enter **200** in the Maximum text box.

4. To specify a message to appear after a user clicks an input cell, click the Input Message tab and type a message in the Input Message text box. If you want a title to appear at the top of the message, enter a title in the Title text box.

   Following the example that we gave in Step 3, you might type the message **Enter a value between 100 and 200**, which appears after the user clicks the cell.

5. To specify a custom error message to appear in a dialog box if someone enters invalid data, click the Error Alert tab and type a message in the Error Message text box. If you want a title to appear at the top of the message, enter a title in the Title text box.

   Following the example that we gave in Step 3, you might type the message **Please enter a value between 100 and 200**, which appears in a dialog box if the user enters invalid data in a cell.

   Choose a style for the error message from the Style drop-down list box (Stop, Warning, or Information). Each style that you select displays an error icon and various buttons on the error dialog box as follows:

   - Stop: Displays Retry and Cancel buttons.

   - Warning: Displays Yes, No, and Cancel buttons. (Clicking Yes enters the invalid data.)

   - Information: Displays OK and Cancel buttons. (Clicking OK enters the invalid data.)

6. Click OK.

If you subsequently want to remove the validation criteria from a cell or range, select the cell or range, click the upper portion of the Data Validation split button in the Ribbon's Data tab, and click the Clear All button in the Data Validation dialog box that appears.

Remember: If you don't specify a message in Step 5, Excel uses a default message if a data-entry error occurs.

You can combine data validation with worksheet protection to permit only validated input cells to be altered. *See* "Protecting a Worksheet," in Part 3.

Part 5

Using Formulas and Functions

This part deals with topics related to formulas and functions. Formulas make using spreadsheets valuable by allowing you to calculate results from data stored in the worksheet. Functions are built-in or custom tools used in formulas. They can make your formulas perform powerful feats and save you a great deal of time.

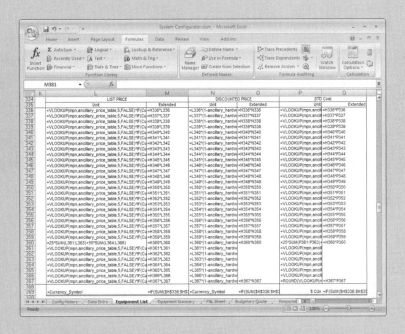

In this part . . .

- ✔ **Absolute, Relative, and Mixed References**
- ✔ **Converting Formulas to Values**
- ✔ **Entering Functions in Formulas**
- ✔ **Referencing Cells or Ranges in Other Worksheets**

Absolute, Relative, and Mixed References

If you copy a formula containing an *absolute reference,* Excel doesn't adjust the reference in the copied cell. (An absolute reference uses two dollar signs in its address, one for the column part and one for the row part.) On the other hand, Excel adjusts *relative references* as you copy the formula.

Excel also enables you to use *mixed references,* in which only one of the address's parts is absolute. The following table summarizes all the possible types of cell references.

Type	Example
Relative reference	A1
Absolute reference	$A$1
Mixed reference (column part is absolute)	$A1
Mixed reference (row part is absolute)	A$1

To change the type of cell reference in a formula, follow these steps:

1. Double-click the cell containing the formula (or press F2) to get into Edit mode.

2. In the cell or formula bar, click the mouse pointer on the cell reference.

3. Press F4 repeatedly to cycle through all possible cell reference types. Stop after the cell reference displays the correct type.

4. Press Enter to complete the operation.

Basic Formula Essentials

In Excel 2007, a formula can consist of up to 8,192 characters (up from 1,024 characters in earlier versions) and any of the following elements:

- ✔ Operators such as + (for addition) and * (for multiplication)

- ✔ Cell references (including named cells and ranges)

- ✔ Values, text, or logical values

- ✔ Worksheet functions (such as SUM or AVERAGE)

After you enter a formula into a cell, the cell displays the result of the formula. You see the formula itself in the *formula bar* as the cell activates. (The formula bar lies below the Ribbon.)

Operator precedence is the set of rules that Excel uses to perform its calculations in a formula.

The following table provides the list of operators that you can use in formulas and indicates each operator's precedence.

Operator	Name	Precedence
^	Exponentiation (raised to a power)	1
*	Multiplication	2
/	Division	2
+	Addition	3
–	Subtraction	3
&	Concatenation (joins text)	4
=	Equal to	5
>	Greater than	5
<	Less than	5

The table shows that exponentiation has the highest precedence (that is, Excel performs it first), and logical comparisons have the lowest precedence. If two operators have the same precedence, Excel performs the calculations from left to right.

Remember: You can override operator precedence by using parentheses in your formulas. In the formula =(Income-Expenses)*TaxRate, for example, Expenses are subtracted from Income, and the result is multiplied by TaxRate.

Changing When Formulas Are Calculated

If the Excel calculation mode is set to automatic (the default), changing cells that you use in a formula causes the formula to display a new result automatically.

To set the Excel calculation mode to manual, click the Formulas tab on the Ribbon, click the Options button in the Calculation group, and choose Manual from the menu.

Remember: If you're working in manual calculation mode, Excel displays Calculate in the status bar if you have any uncalculated formulas. Do the following to recalculate the formulas:

  ✔ Click the Formulas tab on the Ribbon and click the Calculate Now button in the Calculation group or press F9. The formulas in all open workbooks are immediately calculated.

✔ Click the Formulas tab on the Ribbon and click the Calculate Sheet button in the Calculation group or press Shift+F9. The formulas in the active worksheet only are immediately calculated. Other worksheets in the same workbook aren't calculated.

Remember: The Excel calculation mode isn't specific to a particular worksheet. If you change the calculation mode, that change affects all open workbooks and not just the active workbook.

To return to automatic calculation mode, click the Formulas tab on the Ribbon, click the Options button in the Calculation group, and choose Automatic from the menu.

Converting Formulas to Values

Sometimes, you may want to convert a formula to its current value (remove the formula and leave only its result). For example, want may want to prevent future changes to the value of a cell if other cells that the formula references change.

To convert a formula to its current value, follow these steps:

1. Select the cell that contains the formula. To convert several formulas, you can select a range.

2. Click the Copy button on the Ribbon's Home tab. (You can also press Ctrl+C or right-click the cell and choose Copy from the contextual menu.)

3. Click the bottom part of the Paste button on the Ribbon's Home tab (the part with the downward pointing arrow) and choose Paste Values from the menu.

4. Press Enter or Esc to cancel Copy mode.

Remember: The preceding procedure overwrites the formulas. To put the current values of the formulas in a different (empty) area of the worksheet, select a different cell or range before Step 3.

Editing Functions in Formulas

After you create a formula with one or more functions, you may want to modify the arguments in one of the functions later. Excel provides several ways for you to modify a function. The method you choose depends on personal choice and the complexity of the function.

Use any of the following techniques to modify a function:

✔ If your formula contains only one function or if the function you want to modify is the last one in the formula, click the Insert Function button on the formula bar (or in the Formulas tab of the Ribbon), or press Shift+F3 to display the Insert Function dialog box for the function.

✔ If your formula contains more than one function, press F2 or double-click the formula cell. Position the cursor within the function that you want to modify and click the Insert Function button, or press Shift+F3.

✔ The most efficient way to modify simple functions (that is, those with few arguments) is to do so manually. Excel provides a ScreenTip (floating text) for the function to help you identify the names and order of the function's arguments.

See also "Entering Functions in Formulas," immediately following this section.

Entering Functions in Formulas

Excel provides more than 300 built-in functions that can make your formulas perform powerful feats and save you a great deal of time. Functions perform the following tasks:

✔ Simplify your formulas

✔ Enable formulas to perform calculations that are otherwise impossible

✔ Enable conditional execution of formulas — giving them some rudimentary decision-making capability

Most worksheet functions use one or more arguments, enclosed in parentheses. Think of an argument as a piece of information that clarifies what you want the function to do. For example, the following function (which rounds the number in cell A1 to two decimal places) uses two arguments:

=ROUND(A1,2)

Remember: You can *nest* a function within another function. The formula =SUM(MAX(B1:B6),ROUND(A1,2)), for example, nests the MAX and ROUND functions in the SUM function.

See also "Editing Functions in Formulas," immediately preceding this section.

Entering functions manually

Even if you're not familiar with the function that you want to use, you can begin typing the function name and Excel's Formula AutoComplete feature will drop-down a list of possible matches, as shown in Figure 5-1.

Figure 5-1

If you continue typing without selecting a name from the list, Excel narrows the available choices. If you want to select a function name from the list, you can either double-click with the mouse or highlight the name (using the mouse or arrow keys) and press the Tab key. Excel inserts the function in the formula and includes an opening parenthesis.

Excel provides assistance for the functions in the drop-down list in the form of ScreenTips (see Figure 5-1.) Each ScreenTip provides a brief description of the function's use.

Excel provides you with further assistance after you type the entire function name manually (including the opening parenthesis) or you select the function from the drop-down list. This assistance enables you to determine the number and order of arguments in the function. Excel displays a ScreenTip below the function you're typing. The ScreenTip includes the name of the function you typed followed by the names of all the function's mandatory and optional arguments in parentheses. To display a Help window for the function, click the function name in the ScreenTip.

See also "Entering formulas manually," in Part 4.

Using the AutoSum tool

The AutoSum tool provides a quick method for you to enter some functions that you commonly use.

To use the AutoSum tool, follow these steps:

   1. Click a cell below or to the right of a range of numbers.

2. Perform one of the following actions:

   - To sum the range, click the AutoSum button in the Ribbon's Home tab or Formulas tab. Excel places a *marquee* around cells that it thinks you want to sum. If the range of cells that the marquee surrounds isn't the range that you want to sum, use the mouse to highlight a new range. Click the AutoSum button again or press Enter to complete the operation.

   - To find the average, count, minimum, or maximum of the range, click the arrow on the AutoSum button to display a menu for selecting these operations. Click the operation that you want to perform from the menu, and follow the procedure that we describe for summing the range after Excel places the marquee around the cells.

TIP

Excel automatically places a marquee around the first region that it encounters above or to the left of the formula cell. A *region* is a range that contains non-blank cells. To select multiple regions as you use the AutoSum tool in Step 2, press and hold Ctrl while dragging the mouse over each region. ***See also*** "Selecting Cells and Ranges," in Part 4.

Using the Function Library

The Function Library enables you to easily enter a function and its arguments. The Function Library is particularly useful if you're not sure of the function you're looking for and want to browse through the available choices. To make it easier to find what you're looking for, Excel groups the available functions into well-known categories, such as financial and text.

To enter a function by using the Function Library, follow these steps:

1. Activate the cell that will contain the function. If you're inserting the function into an existing formula, click the formula at the position where you want to insert the function.

2. If you're inserting a new function adjacent to another function in a formula, you must add an operator (for example, +, −, or *) at this point to delimit the two functions.

3. Click the Formulas tab on the Ribbon and click a function category in the Function Library group. You can click the More Functions button if the category you want is not shown in the Functions Library group.

4. Choose a function that you want from the menu. Excel displays the Function Arguments dialog box, as shown in Figure 5-2. The Function Arguments dialog box prompts you for each argument of the function that you select. You can enter the arguments manually, or you can point to them in the worksheet if they're cell references. The Function Arguments dialog box displays the result.

To get help with the function, click Help on This Function in the Function Arguments dialog box. Excel displays the Help window for the function.

5. After you specify all the required arguments, click OK.

Figure 5-2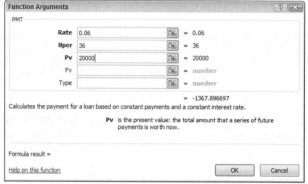

Modifying a Range Reference Used in a Function

If you edit a cell that contains a formula, Excel color-codes the references in the formula and places an outline around each cell or range that the formula references. The color of the outline corresponds to the color that appears in the formula. Each outlined cell or range also contains *fill handles* (a small square in each corner of the outlined cell or range). See Figure 5-3.

Figure 5-3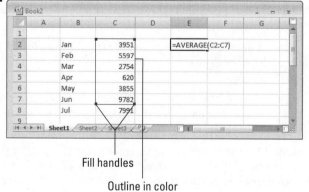

Fill handles

Outline in color

If your formula contains a function that uses a range argument, you can easily modify the range reference by following these steps:

1. To begin editing the formula, press F2 or double-click the cell. ***See also*** "Editing the Contents of a Cell," in Part 4.

2. Locate the range that the function uses. (The range appears with an outline.)

3. Drag a fill handle to extend or contract the range. You can also click a border of the outlined range and move the outline to a new range. In either case, Excel changes the range reference in the formula.

4. Press Enter.

Remember: Formulas that contain name references place a colored outline around the named cell or range. The outline doesn't provide fill handles, however, or enable you to move this type of reference by clicking a border of the outline.

Referencing Cells or Ranges in Other Worksheets

If your formula needs to refer to a cell in a different worksheet in the same workbook, use the following format for your formula:

`SheetName!CellAddress`

Remember: If the worksheet name in the reference includes one or more spaces, you must enclose it in single quotation marks. The following is a formula that refers to a cell on a sheet by the name of All Depts:

`=A1*'All Depts'!A1`

An easy way to enter a range reference on another worksheet is by pointing with the mouse. ***See*** "Entering formulas by pointing," in Part 4.

If you need to reference a 3-D range in a function, enter the range in the following format:

`=FunctionName(FirstSheet:LastSheet!RangeReference)`

For example:

`=SUM(Sheet2:Sheet4!$A$1:$A$10)`

The following rules apply to 3-D range references:

- ✔ The range includes all sheets between the first and last sheet names in the reference, inclusive.

- ✔ If you insert another sheet between the first and last sheets, it will be included in the reference automatically.

- ✔ You can use absolute or relative references in the range reference.

- ✔ You can use any valid names for the sheets, but if any name has a space, you must use single quotes to enclose the names in the reference. For example:

```
=SUM('Dept Engineering:Dept HR'!$A$1:$A$10)
```

Remember: Less than 10 percent of Excel's functions support 3-D range references and those that do fall mostly in the statistical category.

 You can point with the mouse to create a 3-D reference. First position the mouse in the function where the reference will be placed. Then select the cell or range in the first worksheet that will be included in the reference. Next, press and hold Shift and click the sheet tab of the last sheet in the reference. Press Enter to complete the procedure.

Part 6

Creating and Using Names

Dealing with cryptic cell and range addresses can be confusing. Fortunately, Excel enables you to assign descriptive names to cells and ranges. For example, you can name a cell `InterestRate` or name a range `JulySales`.

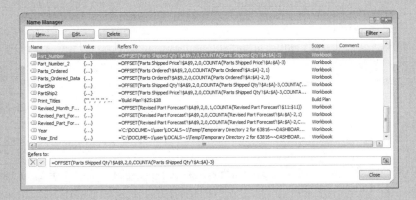

In this part . . .

- ✔ **Applying Names to Existing Cell References**
- ✔ **Creating, Deleting, and Editing Names**
- ✔ **Managing Names**
- ✔ **Naming Constants and Formulas**
- ✔ **Pasting Names into a Formula**

Advantages to Naming Cells and Ranges

Using names for cells and ranges offers the following advantages:

✓ A meaningful range name (such as Income) is much easier to remember than a range address (such as A1:A21).

✓ After you select a named cell or range, its name appears in the name box.

✓ You can quickly move to a named area of your worksheet by choosing a name in the name box.

✓ Creating formulas is easier, because you can paste a cell or range name into a formula.

✓ Names make your formulas more understandable and easier to use. For example, =Income-Taxes is more intuitive than =D20-D40.

Although Excel is flexible about the names that you can define, it does have the following rules:

✓ Names must begin with a letter or the underscore character (_).

✓ Names can't contain any spaces. You may want to use an underscore or a period character to simulate a space (such as Annual_Total or Annual.Total).

✓ You can use any combination of letters and numbers, but the name must not begin with a number (such as 3rdQuarter) or look like a cell reference (such as Q3).

✓ You can't use most symbols. You can, however, use the underscore (_), period (.), backslash (\), and question mark (?).

✓ Names can be no more than 255 characters long.

Excel also reserves a few names internally for its own use. Avoid using the following for names: Print_Area, Print_Titles, Consolidate_Area, and Sheet_Title.

Applying Names to Existing Cell References

If you create a new name for a cell or a range, Excel doesn't automatically use the name in place of existing references in your formulas. For example, if you have a formula such as =A1*20 and then give a name to cell A1, the formula continues to display A1 (not the new name). Replacing cell or range references with their corresponding names, however, is fairly easy.

To apply names to cell references in existing formulas, follow these steps:

1. Select the range with the formulas that you want to modify.

2. Click the Formulas tab on the Ribbon, click the arrow on the Define Name button, and choose Apply Names from the menu. Excel displays the Apply Names dialog box, as shown in Figure 6-1.

Figure 6-1

3. Select the names that you want to apply by clicking them in turn.

4. Click OK. Excel replaces the range references with the names in the selected cells.

TIP

If you select a nonformula cell in Step 1, Excel applies the names to all applicable formulas in the worksheet.

Creating Names

Excel provides several useful methods for creating names. The method you choose depends on personal preference and techniques that may allow you to save time.

Creating a name using the New Name dialog box

To create a range name using the New Name dialog box, follow these steps:

1. Select the cell or range that you want to name.

2. Click the Formulas tab on the Ribbon and then click the Define Name button (or right-click the range and choose Name a Range from the contextual menu). Excel displays the New Name dialog box, as shown in Figure 6-2.

3. In the Name text box, type a name (or use the name that Excel proposes, if any).

4. If needed, enter a comment in the Comment box. You can enter a comment, for example, to provide a description and other details of the name for future worksheet auditing purposes.

5. Verify that the address Excel displays in the Refers To text box is correct. To refer to a different address, delete the address and then either type the new cell or range address (with a leading equal sign) or use the mouse pointer to select the cell or range on the worksheet.

6. Click OK.

Figure 6-2

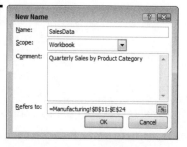

If you want to create several names in one go, use the Name Manager instead of the Define Name method. Click the Name Manager button in the Formulas tab. In the Name Manager dialog box, click New to add a name. After you finish adding a name, you're returned to the Name Manager dialog box, where you can repeat the process to create additional names.

Creating a name using the name box

The name box is on the left side of the formula bar, as shown in Figure 6-3.

Name box   Name box divider

Figure 6-3

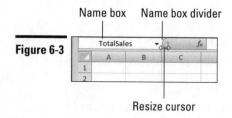

Resize cursor

To create a name by using the name box, follow these steps:

1. Select the cell or range to name.

2. Click the name box, and enter the name.

3. Press Enter to create the name.

Remember: If a name already exists, you can't use the name box to change the reference for the name. Attempting to do so simply displays the already existing name.

Excel 2007 allows you to increase the width of the name box, so that you can see more of longer names. Drag the name box divider (the area around the dimple in Figure 6-3) to the left or right.

Creating names from row and column labels

Your worksheet may contain column or row labels that you want to use for naming adjacent cells or ranges. Figure 6-4 shows a range of data with month labels in the left column and regions on the top row. You can create a name for each row in the range using the labels in the left column or create a name for each column in the range using the labels in the top row. You can also use both top row and left column to name simultaneously each row and each column in the range.

Figure 6-4

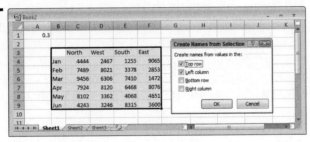

To create names by using adjacent row or column labels, follow these steps:

1. Select the name labels and the cells that you want to name. (These can be individual cells or ranges of cells.) The labels must be adjacent to the cells that you're naming. A multiple selection isn't possible here.

2. Click the Formulas tab on the Ribbon and then click the Create from Selection button. The Create Names from Selection dialog box appears. Excel guesses how to create the names by checking the appropriate Create Names From Values In The check boxes. If the labels are on the left of the cells that you want to name, for example, Excel selects the Left Column option.

3. If Excel's selection isn't what you want, clear the selection and select the correct Create Names From Values In The check boxes as necessary.

4. Click OK to create the names.

If you create names from both row and column labels, you can refer to an entry in your table by the intersection of the row and column labels. In Figure 6-4, for example, I created names from the top row and left column labels in the range. You can create a formula like this: `=A1*Mar North`, where `Mar North` = 9456.

Remember: If the label that a cell contains results in an invalid name, Excel modifies the name to make it valid. If Excel encounters a value or a formula where a text label should be, however, it doesn't convert it to a valid name. It simply doesn't create a name.

Remember: The names that you create do *not* include the cells with the labels.

Creating sheet-level names

Normally, you can use a name that you create anywhere within the workbook. Names, by default, are book-level rather than sheet-level in *scope*. But what if you have several worksheets in a workbook and you want to use the same name (such as `Dept_Total`) in each sheet to signify different values? You need to create sheet-level names.

To define a sheet-level name, follow these steps:

1. Complete Steps 1–5 in the procedure for "Creating a name using the New Name dialog box," earlier in this part.

2. Click the Scope drop-down list and select the sheet name to which the name you're defining will belong. Although you can select any sheet name from the list, you'll normally want to choose the sheet with your selected cell or range.

3. Click OK.

You also can create a sheet-level name by using the name box. Select the cell or range, click the name box, and enter the name, preceding it with the sheet's name (surrounded with single quotes if the name contains spaces) and an exclamation point. For example, if you want to create a sheet-level name of `Dept_Total` in a sheet named `Human Resources`, enter `'Human Resources'!Dept_Total` in the name box.

Remember: If you write a formula that uses a sheet-level name on the sheet where you define it, you don't need to include the worksheet name in the range name. (The name box doesn't display the worksheet name either.) If you use the name in a formula on a different worksheet, however, you must use the entire name (sheet name, exclamation point, and name).

Creating multisheet names

Names can extend into the third dimension — across multiple worksheets in a workbook. Multisheet names must include contiguous worksheets and must refer to the same cell or range reference in each worksheet. To create a multisheet name, follow these steps:

1. Click the Formulas tab on the Ribbon and then click the Define Name button. Excel displays the New Name dialog box.

2. In the Name text box, type a name (or use the name that Excel proposes, if any).

3. In the Refers To text box, enter the reference (and remember to begin it with an equal sign). The format for a multisheet reference is

   ```
   FirstSheet:LastSheet!RangeReference
   ```

4. Click OK.

An easier way to enter the reference in Step 3 is by pointing. Follow these steps after Step 2 (of the preceding list) to create a multisheet reference by pointing:

1. Click the tab of the first worksheet in the range, if it isn't already selected.

2. Click the Refers To text box, and delete the suggested reference (which usually isn't the one you want).

3. Press and hold Shift, and click the tab of the last worksheet that you want to include in the reference.

4. Select the cell or range in the first worksheet that you want to include in the name reference. The Refers To text box displays the multisheet range.

5. Click OK.

Deleting Names

If you no longer need a defined name, you can delete it by following these steps:

1. Click the Formulas tab on the Ribbon and then click the Name Manager button. Excel displays the Name Manager dialog box.

2. In the list, select the name that you want to delete and then click the Delete button. Excel asks you to confirm the deletion.

3. Click OK to delete.

If you change your mind after deleting the name, Excel 2007 allows you to undo the deletion. Click the Undo button on the Quick Access toolbar or press Ctrl+Z. Earlier versions of Excel don't allow you to undo a name deletion.

4. Select another name to delete or click Close the exit the Name Manager dialog box.

Be careful when deleting names. If you use the name in a formula, deleting the name causes the formula to become invalid. (Excel displays #NAME?.)

If you delete the rows or columns that contain named cells or ranges, the names contain an invalid reference. For example, if cell A1 on Sheet1 is named Interest and you delete row 1 or column A, Interest then refers to =Sheet1!#REF! (that is, an erroneous reference). If you use the name Interest in a formula, the formula displays #REF.

Editing Names

Editing names in Excel 2007 is simple with the new Name Manager. You can modify the name, scope, comment, or reference. Follow these steps to edit a name in the workbook:

1. Click the Formulas tab on the Ribbon and then click the Name Manager button. Excel displays the Name Manager dialog box.

2. In the list, select the name you want to change and then click the Edit button. Excel displays the Edit Name dialog box.

3. Enter a new name, comment, reference, or scope for the name and then click OK.

4. Select another name to edit or click Close to exit the dialog box.

Managing Names

It's not unusual for a workbook to contain several dozen, hundreds, or even thousands of defined names. This situation makes tasks such as deleting multiple names, renaming names, and finding broken names challenging. Excel 2007 provides a Name Manager dialog box that you can use to view and manage the defined names in a workbook, as shown in Figure 6-5. To display the Name Manager dialog box, click the Formulas tab on the Ribbon and then click the Name Manager button.

Figure 6-5

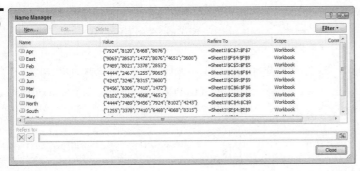

Using the Name Manager dialog, you can

- ✔ View information for existing defined names, such as name, value, scope, reference, and comment. **See also** "Creating sheet-level names," earlier in this part, for a discussion of a name's scope.

- ✔ Create new names by clicking the New button to display the New Name dialog box.

- ✔ Edit existing names by selecting the name and clicking the Edit button to display the Edit Name dialog box.

- ✔ Delete multiple names at once by selecting the names (hold down Shift or Ctrl to select the names) and clicking the Delete button.

- ✔ Sort any column by clicking on the column header.

- ✔ Resize the dialog box (by dragging any edge of the dialog box) so that you can see more names and longer references in the Refers To box.

- ✔ Filter the list of names based on common criteria by clicking the Filter button and selecting an option from the menu. The menu is separated into three filter categories and you can select (through successive mouse clicks) an option in each category.

Naming Constants and Formulas

Names that you use in Excel don't need to refer to a cell or a range. You can give a name to a constant or even to a formula. If formulas in your worksheet refer to an interest rate (such as .085, or 8.5 percent), for example, you can define a name for this particular constant and then use it in your formulas. Alternatively, you can create a name that refers to a formula such as =SUM($A$1:$A$10) and use the name in your worksheet formulas.

To define a name for a constant or formula, follow these steps:

1. Click the Formulas tab on the Ribbon and then click the Define Name button. Excel displays the New Name dialog box.

2. In the Name text box, type a name for the constant or formula.

3. If needed, enter a comment in the Comment box. You can enter a comment, for example, to provide a description of the name for future worksheet auditing purposes.

4. In the Refers To text box, enter the value for the constant or the expression for the formula. Normally, this field holds a cell or range reference, but you can also enter a value or formula.

5. Click OK.

After performing these steps, you can use the name in your formulas.

Pasting Names into a Formula

If your formula uses named cells or ranges, you can type the name in place of the address. Another approach is to select the name from a list and have Excel insert the name for you automatically at your cursor location in the formula. You can do so in two ways:

✔ Click the Formulas tab on the Ribbon, click the Use in Formula button, and then select a name from the list.

✔ Press F3 to display the Paste Name dialog box, select a name from the list, and click OK.

Part 7

Auditing Your Work

When your worksheets begin to get larger and more complex, ensuring accuracy becomes more difficult. That's why, for all but the most basic spreadsheets, auditing is an important task. *Auditing* refers to the process of tracking down and identifying errors in your worksheet. Excel provides a set of interactive auditing tools and other tools that are useful in the auditing process, although they are not dedicated to this purpose.

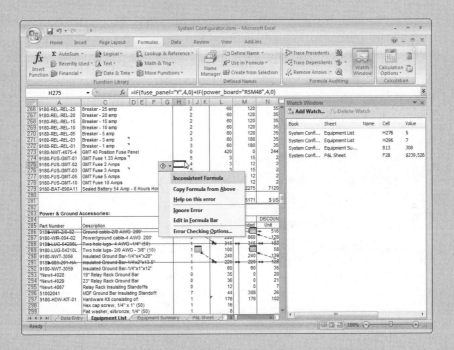

In this part . . .

- ✔ **Checking for Specific Worksheet Errors**
- ✔ **Evaluating Parts of a Formula**
- ✔ **Tracing Cell Relationships**
- ✔ **Understanding Formula Error Values**
- ✔ **Using the Watch Window**

Checking for Specific Worksheet Errors

Excel can alert you regarding specific types of errors or potential errors in your worksheet. Excel can flag the following types of errors:

✔ Formulas that evaluate to error values (for example, `#DIV/0!`, `#VALUE!`, or `#N/A`)

✔ Text dates (that is, dates you format as text or precede with an apostrophe) that you enter with two-digit years

✔ Numbers that you store as text (that is, numbers that you format as text or precede with an apostrophe)

✔ Inconsistent formulas in a region (that is, different from formulas in surrounding cells)

✔ Formulas that omit cells in a region (for example, a formula that sums a range but omits the last cell or cells in the range)

✔ Unlocked cells that contain formulas if the worksheet is protected

✔ Formulas that contain references to empty cells

Remember: Use Excel's suggestions to serve as a guide to potential errors in your worksheet. Excel may flag as errors data that you enter intentionally.

Excel's error-alert feature isn't foolproof. You should use it with other techniques that we discuss in this part.

Checking for errors in the background

By default, Excel checks for worksheet errors in the background. If it identifies an error or a potential error, Excel displays an indicator in the upper-left corner of the offending cell. After you click the cell, Excel displays the Error Warning Smart Tag on the left side of the offending cell. If you hover the mouse pointer over the Error Warning Smart Tag, Excel displays a message that indicates the nature of the error, as shown in Figure 7-1.

Figure 7-1

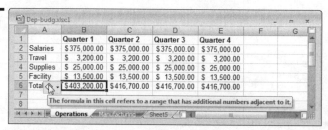

To correct the error or to tell Excel to ignore it, click the Error Warning Smart Tag and select an option from the drop-down list that appears.

See also "Checking for errors manually," immediately following this section.

Checking for errors manually

You may want to avoid the distraction of Excel's automatic worksheet error checking and perform the error-checking task manually after you complete work on your spreadsheet model.

To turn off background error checking, follow these steps:

1. Click the Office button and then click the Excel Options button. Excel displays the Excel Options dialog box with a list of option sections in the left pane.

2. Click the Formulas section.

3. Clear the Enable Background Error Checking check box.

4. Click OK.

To check for worksheet errors manually, follow these steps:

1. Select the worksheet that you want to check for errors.

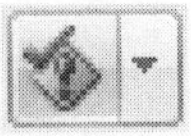

2. Click the Formulas tab on the Ribbon and then click the Error Checking button in the Formula Auditing group. Excel displays the Error Checking dialog box and places the cell pointer in the first cell that it encounters containing an error or potential error. The dialog box indicates the nature of the error that you encounter in the cell, as shown in Figure 7-2.

Figure 7-2

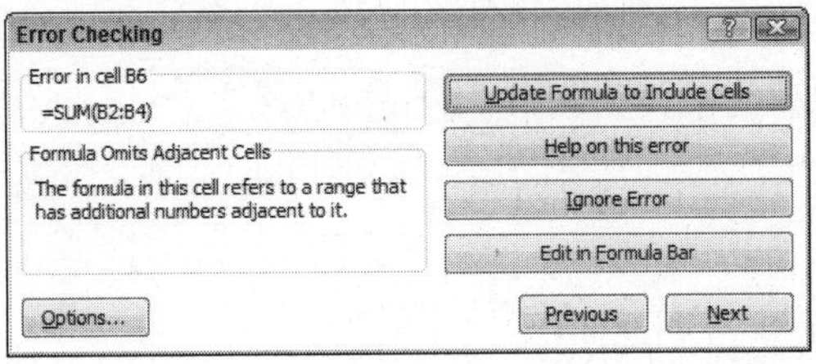

3. Click one of the four option buttons on the right side of the dialog box.

4. Click Next to move to the next cell that contains an error or a potential error.

An alternative to this procedure is to turn on background error checking *after* your spreadsheet model is complete and use the procedure in "Checking for errors in the background," immediately preceding this section, for each cell that Excel flags with an error.

You can control the types of errors that you want Excel to consider (automatically or through the manual procedure). Click the Office button and then click the Excel Options button. Click the Formulas section on the left pane of the dialog box, and select or clear the options in the Error Checking Rules area.

Checking Your Spelling

Excel uses a spell checker that works just like the feature you find in word-processing programs. You can access the spell checker by using either of the following methods:

- Click the Review tab on the Ribbon and then click the Spelling button
- Press F7

The extent of the spell checking depends on what you select before you access the dialog box.

What You Select	What Excel Checks
A single cell	The entire worksheet, including cell contents, notes, text in graphic objects and charts, and page headers and footers
A range of cells	Only that range
A group of characters	Only the characters in the formula bar

If Excel encounters a word that isn't in the current dictionary or is misspelled, it offers a list of suggestions that you can click to respond to.

Creating a Table of Names

You can create a list of all the names and associated name references in the workbook. This procedure may be useful for tracking down errors or as a way to document your work.

To create a table of names, follow these steps:

1. Move the cell pointer to an empty area of your worksheet or add a new worksheet. (Excel creates the table at the active cell position.)

2. Click the Formulas tab on the Ribbon, click the arrow on the Use in Formula button, and then select the Paste option at the bottom of the list. (Or simply press F3.) Excel displays the Paste Name dialog box.

3. Click the Paste List button and Excel creates your table of names.

 The list that Excel pastes overwrites any cells that get in the way, so make sure the active cell is in an empty portion of the worksheet.

Displaying Formulas in a Worksheet

One way to audit your workbook is to display the formulas rather than the results of the formulas. Then you can examine the formulas without needing to select cells individually.

 To display formulas instead of formula results, click the Formulas tab on the Ribbon and then click the Show Formulas button in the Formula Auditing group. (You can also press Ctrl+~.)

 You may want to create a new window for the workbook before issuing this command. That way, you can see the formulas in one window and the results in the other. *See also* "Creating Multiple Windows (Views) for a Workbook," in Part 2.

Evaluating Parts of a Formula

Excel provides a tool that helps you evaluate (that is, calculate) parts of a formula and trace the precedents of parts of a formula. (*Precedents* are cells that are referenced in the formula part you're evaluating.) The capability to evaluate parts of a formula can prove useful if you're tracking down errors in formulas.

To evaluate parts of a formula, follow these steps:

1. Click the cell that contains the formula.

 2. Click the Formulas tab on the Ribbon and then click the Evaluate Formula button in the Formula Auditing group. Excel displays the Evaluate Formula dialog box. In the Reference area, the cell reference appears. The Evaluation preview box displays the formula with the first expression or cell reference underlined.

3. To show the value of the underlined expression, click Evaluate. Excel italicizes the result of the expression.

4. Repeat Step 3 as many times as necessary to evaluate all expressions in the formula.

5. Use the Step In button to examine the formula that the underlined cell reference in the expression represents. Use the Step Out button to evaluate the current reference and return to the previous reference (see Figure 7-3).

6. Click Close after you finish evaluating the formula.

Figure 7-3

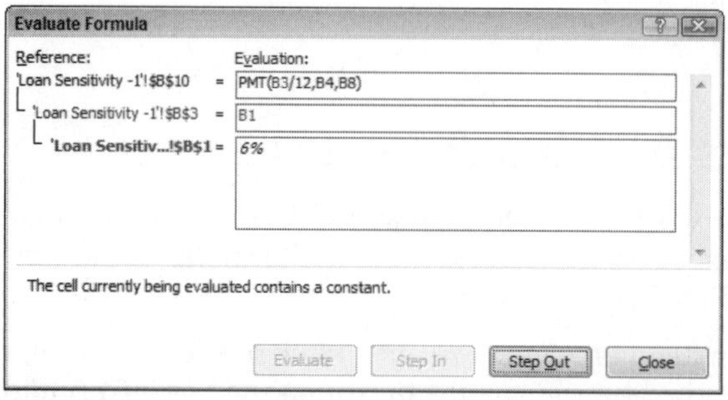

Evaluate Formula	? ✖

Reference:

Evaluation:

'Loan Sensitivity -1'!$B$10 = PMT(B3/12,B4,B8)

'Loan Sensitivity -1'!$B$3 = B1

'Loan Sensitiv...!$B$1 = 6%

The cell currently being evaluated contains a constant.

[Evaluate] [Step In] [**Step Out**] [Close]

Remember: The Step In button is not available if a cell reference lies in a different workbook.

The Evaluate Formula feature is an excellent tool to use when your formula returns an error value because you can examine and correct the part of the formula that is generating the error.

A quick way to evaluate parts of a formula is to go into edit mode (by double-clicking the cell or pressing F2), highlight the part of the formula that you want to evaluate, and press F9. Excel displays the result of the formula part. Press Esc to cancel. Do *not* press Enter; otherwise, Excel permanently replaces the part of the formula with the resulting value.

Finding Specific Data

If your worksheets contain lots of data, you may find locating a particular piece of information difficult. Excel can find the data for you.

To locate a particular value or sequence of text, follow these steps:

1. Click the Find & Select button in the Ribbon's Home tab and choose Find from the menu. (Or simply press Ctrl+F.) Excel displays its Find and Replace dialog box with the Find tab selected, as shown in Figure 7-4.

Figure 7-4

2. In the Find What drop-down list box, enter the characters to search for You can also use the list also to select items that you previously searched for.

3. If you want to make your search case-sensitive, select the Match Case check box. If the Match Case check box isn't visible, click the Options button.

4. To search for data with specific formatting:

   a. Click the Format button. (If the Format button isn't visible, click the Options button.) Excel displays the Find Format dialog box.

   b. Click the appropriate tabs, and in each tab, specify the formatting that you're looking for.

   c. After you complete your selections, click OK.

If a cell in your worksheet already contains all the formatting you want to use in your search, click the arrow on the Format button and select Choose Format From Cell. Excel adds an eyedropper icon to the cursor. Click the cell with the required formatting.

5. In the Within drop-down list box, select whether you want to look in the active sheet or the entire workbook. (If the Within drop-down box isn't visible, click the Options button.)

6. In the Search drop-down box, select the direction that you want to search, as follows:

   • Select By Rows to search across rows.

   • Select By Columns to search down columns.

   In most cases, your search goes faster if you select By Columns.

7. In the Look In drop-down list box, specify what to look in: Formulas, Values, or Comments.

8. Click the Find Next button. Excel selects the cell that contains what you're looking for.

   If you click the Find All button, Excel displays a drop-down window that shows all references to the found data, either in the active worksheet or across the entire workbook, depending on your selection in Step 5. Click a reference in the window to go directly to that cell.

9. Click the Close button to end your search.

For approximate searches, use *wildcard characters.* An asterisk represents any group of characters in the specified position, and a question mark represents any single character in the specified position. If you type **w*h**, for example, those letters represent all text that begins with *w* and ends with *h.* Similarly, **b?n** matches three-letter words such as *bin, bun,* and *ban.*

Remember: To find a cell or cells with specific formatting but containing no specific data, you can skip Step 2.

See also "Searching for Data to Replace," in Part 4.

Handling Circular References

As you enter formulas, you may occasionally see a message from Excel that is similar to the one shown in Figure 7-5. This message indicates that the formula you just entered will result in a circular reference. A *circular reference* occurs if a formula refers to its own value (either directly or indirectly).

Figure 7-5

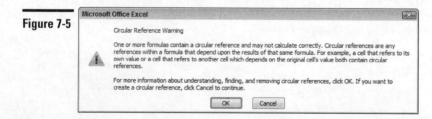

If Excel encounters a circular reference after you enter a formula, a message is displayed that enables you to correct the formula or to enter the formula as is. If you enter a formula with a circular reference, Excel displays a message in the status bar to remind you that a circular reference exists. Most of the time, a circular reference indicates an error that you must correct. In this case, you should click OK after Excel displays the message.

After you click OK in response to the circular reference message, Excel displays direct and indirect *precedent* arrows on the worksheet that loop back to the cell with the circular reference. These arrows help you trace the path of the circular reference. Excel also displays a help window, which provides further assistance for locating circular reference problems. Excel also displays the Help Viewer window, which displays help topics specific to working with circular references.

If you receive a workbook containing circular references, Excel displays a message on the status bar, as mentioned. To correct the problem, follow these steps:

1. Click the Formulas tab on the Ribbon.

2. In the Formula Auditing group, click the arrow on the Error Checking button, and then choose Circular References from the menu. Excel displays a list that includes the cell reference of the cell with the circular reference and the references of any other cells involved in the circular reference (see Figure 7-6).

Figure 7-6

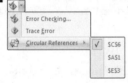

3. Click a cell reference in the list. Excel positions the active cell pointer in the cell.

4. To trace the path of the circular reference, click the Trace Precedents button in the Formulas tab of the Ribbon. Excel displays an arrow on the worksheet that points from the direct precedent of the cell.

5. Click the Trace Precedents button again to add the first indirect precedent of the cell, and so on. Eventually, the precedent arrows loop back to the cell with the circular reference.

The trace precedents technique can be helpful in resolving many circular reference problems.

See also "Tracing Cell Relationships," later in this part.

After you resolve the circular reference problem for a cell, if additional cells have circular reference problems, Excel continues to display the circular reference message on the status bar.

Excel doesn't tell you about a circular reference if the Iteration setting is on. You can check this setting by clicking the Office button, clicking the Excel Options button, and then clicking the Formulas option section in the left pane. The Enable Iterative Calculation option is in the Calculation Options area on the right side of the dialog box. If iteration is on (that is, the Enable Iterative Calculation option is selected), Excel performs the circular calculation the number of times specified in the Maximum Iterations text box (or until the value changes by less than 0.001 — or whatever value is in the Maximum Change text box).

Remember: In a few situations (known by advanced users), a circular reference is intentional. In these cases, the iteration setting must be on. However, it's best to keep the iteration setting off so that Excel warns you of circular references.

Locating Errors by Selecting Special Cells

Excel's ability to select specific types of cells can prove useful in your auditing work. For example, you can select all the cells in the worksheet that contain formulas. (Excel highlights all such cells.) If Excel doesn't select a cell in a region where it highlights other cells (for example, a formula row or column), that situation may indicate that you (or someone else) inadvertently overwrote the cell with a static value.

Follow these steps to select cells that meet your criterion:

1. Click the Find & Select button on the Ribbon's Home tab and then choose an option in the middle part of the menu. The choices are Formulas, Comments, Conditional Formatting, Constants, and Data Validation. Excel highlights all the cells matching the criterion you choose.

2. For additional criteria choices:

   a. Choose Go To Special on the Find & Select button menu. Excel displays the Go To Special dialog box.

   b. Select an option in the Go To Special dialog box.

   c. To get help on the options in the dialog box, click the Help button (the question mark icon) in the dialog box title bar. Excel displays a help window. Click OK to close the window.

3. Click OK. Excel selects all cells that match your selected criteria.

To get an overall view of the worksheet structure if you're selecting special cells and to aid in tracking down potential errors, zoom out the worksheet to a small size. **See** "Zooming a Worksheet," in Part 3.

Excel has some shortcut keys that you can use to select precedent and dependent cells without needing to use the Go To Special dialog box.

Key Combination	*What It Selects*
Ctrl+[	Direct precedents
Ctrl+Shift+[	All precedents
Ctrl+]	Direct dependents
Ctrl+Shift+]	All dependents

See also "Tracing Cell Relationships," next.

Tracing Cell Relationships

Excel's auditing tools can help you track down errors in your worksheet by drawing arrows (known as *cell tracers*) to precedent and dependent cells. A cell's *direct precedents* are cells that are referenced in the cell's formula. An *indirect precedent* is a cell that isn't used directly in the formula but is used by a cell that you refer to in the formula. A cell's *dependents* are formulas that reference the particular cell, either directly or indirectly.

Tracing precedents and dependents

To trace the precedents or dependents of a cell, follow these steps:

1. Click the cell that you want to trace.

2. Click the Formulas tab on the Ribbon and do one of the following:

    - Click the Trace Precedents button in the Formula Auditing group. Excel draws arrows from all *direct* precedent cells.

    - Click the Trace Dependents button in the Formula Auditing group. Excel draws arrows to all *direct* dependent cells. See an example in Figure 7-7.

3. Repeat Step 2 (click the Trace Precedent or Trace Dependent button) as often as necessary to draw arrows to *indirect* precedent or *indirect* dependent cells.

Figure 7-7

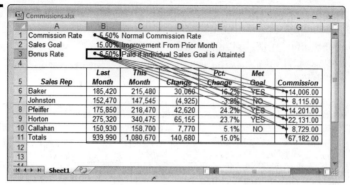

4. Double-click an arrow to move the cell pointer to a precedent cell or a dependent cell. If Excel displays a dashed line pointing to a miniature sheet icon, the precedent cells are on a different worksheet. Double-clicking the dashed line displays the Go To dialog box. Click a cell reference in the Go To dialog box, and click OK.

5. Click the Formulas tab on the Ribbon (if necessary) and then click the Remove Arrows button in the Formula Auditing group after you finish tracing the source of your error.

 TIP If you are developing a large worksheet, this type of interactive tracing is often more revealing if you zoom out of the worksheet to display a larger area. **See** "Zooming a Worksheet," in Part 3.

See also "Tracing formula error values," immediately following this section.

Tracing formula error values

Often, an error in one cell (for example, #DIV/0!, #VALUE!, or #NA) is the result of an error in a precedent cell. Excel helps you to identify the cell or cells that are causing the error value to appear.

To trace the source of the error value, follow these steps:

1. Click the cell that contains the error.

2. Click the Formulas tab on the Ribbon, click the arrow on the Error Checking button in the Formula Auditing group, and choose Trace Error from the menu. Excel draws arrows to all *direct* precedent cells.

3. Repeat Step 2 as often as necessary to draw arrows to *indirect* precedent cells.

4. Double-click an arrow to move the cell pointer to a precedent cell.

5. Click the Formulas tab on the Ribbon (if necessary) and click the Remove Arrows button in the Formula Auditing group after you finish tracing the source of your error.

See also "Understanding Formula Error Values," which appears next, and "Tracing precedents and dependents," earlier in this section.

Understanding Formula Error Values

Excel flags errors in formulas with a message that begins with a pound sign (#). This flag signals that the formula is returning an error value. You must correct the formula (or correct a cell that the formula references) to get rid of the error display.

Remember: If the entire cell is full of pound signs, the column isn't wide enough to display the value (whether or not the value is an error).

The following table lists the types of error values that may appear in a cell that contains a formula.

Error Value	Explanation
#DIV/0!	The formula is trying to divide by zero (an operation that's not allowed on this planet). This error also occurs if the formula attempts to divide by an empty cell.
#NAME?	The formula uses a name that Excel doesn't recognize. This error can happen if you delete a name that the formula uses or if you have unmatched quotes when using text.
#N/A	The error will occur, for example, if the formula refers (directly or indirectly) to a cell that uses #N/A or the NA() function to signal that data is not available. The error might also appear if a required argument is omitted from a worksheet function. A complete discussion of all the possible causes of this error is beyond the scope of this book.
#NULL!	The formula uses an intersection of two ranges that don't intersect.
#NUM!	You have a problem with a value; for example, you're specifying a negative number where Excel expects a positive number.
#REF!	The formula refers to a cell that isn't valid. This error can happen if you've deleted the cell from the worksheet.
#VALUE!	The formula contains a function with an invalid argument, or the formula uses an operand of the wrong type (such as text where Excel expects a value).

Remember: A single error value can make its way to lots of other cells that contain formulas that depend on the cell.

See also "Tracing formula error values," earlier in this part.

Using Cell Comments

The Excel Cell Comment feature enables you to attach a comment to a cell. Comments are useful for documenting a particular value, providing input instructions for users, or helping you remember what a formula does. After you move the mouse pointer over a cell that has a comment, the comment appears in a small box (see Figure 7-8).

Figure 7-8

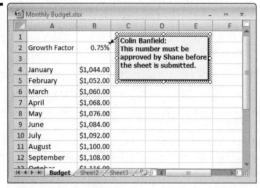

Adding a cell comment

To add a comment to a cell, follow these steps:

1. Select the cell.

2. Click the Review tab on the Ribbon and then click the New Comment button. (You can also right-click the cell and choose New Comment from the contextual menu, or press Shift+F2.)

3. In the text box, enter the text for the comment.

4. After you finish, click any cell.

The cell displays a small red triangle to indicate that it contains a comment.

Editing a cell comment

To edit a comment, follow these steps:

1. Select the cell containing the comment.

2. Click the Review tab on the Ribbon and then click the Edit Comment button. (You can also right-click the cell and choose Edit Comment from the contextual menu, or press Shift+F2.)

3. Edit your comment in the text box displayed.

4. After you finish, click any cell.

Viewing cell comments

Cells to which you attach a comment display a small red triangle in the upper-right corner. After you move the mouse pointer over a cell that contains a comment, Excel displays the comment.

To view the all the comments in the worksheet, click the Review tab on the Ribbon and then click the Show All Comments button. Click Show All Comments again to remove the comment display.

TIP

Zoom out of your worksheet to view more comments. **_See_** "Zooming a Worksheet," in Part 3.

Using the Watch Window

If you're attempting to track down certain problems with large spreadsheet models, the capability to display a window that shows the value of the formula cells if their associated precedents are in different parts of a worksheet, in different worksheets, or even in different open workbooks comes in handy. For example, this ability can be useful if you're unsure of the results that Excel is generating in certain formula cells after you change the values in precedent cells (that is, the cells that the formula references either directly or indirectly). This way, if you make changes to precedent cells, you can see the result of formulas immediately in the window. Excel provides a *Watch window* to handle these situations.

Displaying and adding cells to the Watch window

To display and add cells to the Watch window, follow these steps:

1. Select the cells that you want to watch.

2. Click the Formulas tab on the Ribbon and then click the Watch Window button in the Formula Auditing group. Excel displays the Watch window.

3. Click Add Watch. Excel displays the Add Watch dialog box, with the cell references that you selected in Step 1 already filled in.

4. Click the Add button. Excel adds the cell references to the Watch window, as shown in Figure 7-9.

Figure 7-9

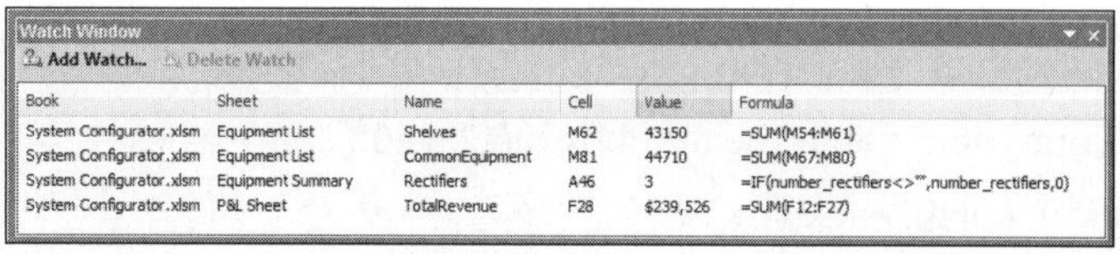

Watch Window					▾ ×
🔍 **Add Watch...** 🔍 Delete Watch					
Book	Sheet	Name	Cell	Value	Formula
System Configurator.xlsm	Equipment List	Shelves	M62	43150	=SUM(M54:M61)
System Configurator.xlsm	Equipment List	CommonEquipment	M81	44710	=SUM(M67:M80)
System Configurator.xlsm	Equipment Summary	Rectifiers	A46	3	=IF(number_rectifiers<>"",number_rectifiers,0)
System Configurator.xlsm	P&L Sheet	TotalRevenue	F28	$239,526	=SUM(F12:F27)

5. To move the active cell pointer to the cell that an entry in the Watch window refers to, double-click the entry in the window.

6. To add cells from other worksheets or open workbooks, switch to the other worksheet or workbook and repeat Steps 1–4.

7. To close or hide the Watch window, click the Close button or click the Watch Window button in the Ribbon's Formula tab.

TIP Instead of closing the Watch window, you can choose to dock it to one side of the screen. Click the title bar of the Watch window and then drag the window to any side of the screen.

To change the width of a column in the Watch window, drag the boundary on the right side of the column heading (the mouse pointer changes to a cross with a double-sided arrow). To resize the Watch window, drag any side of the window (the mouse pointer turns into a double-sided arrow.)

Remember: Cells that contain links to other workbooks appear in the Watch window only if the other workbooks are open.

TIP To select all the cells in a worksheet that contain formulas, do the following: In Step 1 click the Find & Select button on the Ribbon's Home tab, choose Go To Special from the menu, select Formulas in the Go To Special dialog box that appears, and click OK.

Removing cells from the Watch window

To remove cells from the Watch window, follow these steps:

1. Select the cell references in the Watch window that you want to remove. To select contiguous cell references, click the first reference, press and hold Shift, and click the last reference. To select noncontiguous references, press Ctrl and then click the cells.

2. Click Delete Watch.

Part 8

Formatting Your Data

You have a lot of control over the appearance of information that you enter into a cell. Changing the appearance of a cell's content is known as *formatting*. Formatting data in a range can make your worksheet more readable and presentable. In this part, you discover how to apply Excel's many formatting options.

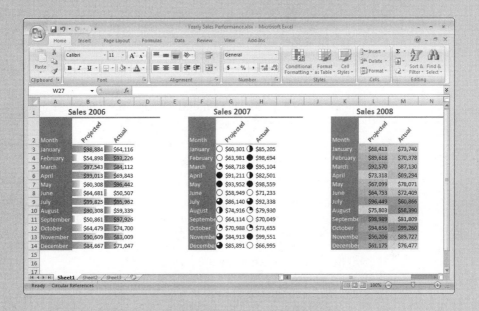

In this part . . .

- ✔ **Changing the Appearance of Cell Contents**
- ✔ **Formatting Based on the Contents of a Cell or Range**
- ✔ **Formatting Numbers**
- ✔ **Formatting Ranges Using Visualizations**
- ✔ **Using Cell Styles**

Adding Borders to a Cell or a Range

People often use borders to group a range of similar cells or simply as a way to delineate rows or columns for aesthetic purposes.

To add borders around a cell or range, follow these steps:

1. Select the cell or range.

2. Click the arrow on the Borders button in the Ribbon's Home tab. Excel displays the Borders menu.

3. Choose a border style from the menu. Excel applies the border to your selection. In addition, the Borders button icon changes to reflect your border selection.

If the available styles on the menu aren't what you want, follow these steps to select further options:

1. At the bottom of the Borders menu, choose More Borders. Excel displays the Format Cells dialog box with the Borders tab selected.

2. If you want to change the default color, choose a color for the border from the Color drop-down palette.

3. In the Style area of the dialog box, select a line style.

4. Select the border position(s) for the line style by clicking in the Text window or by clicking one or more buttons surrounding the Text window. To deselect a line in Text window, click the line. Note that you can apply diagonal borders that extend through cells and ranges. Diagonal borders give the effect of the cells being "crossed out."

5. Click OK to apply the border(s) to your selection.

TIP If you use border formatting in your worksheet, you may want to turn off the grid display to make the borders more pronounced. Click the View tab on the Ribbon and then click the Gridlines option to remove its check mark.

Aligning Cell Contents

Excel's default alignments are such that cell contents appear at the bottom, numbers are right-aligned, text is left-aligned, and logical values (True or False) are centered in cells. You can use Excel's alignment tools to change the default alignments that Excel applies to cell contents. Figure 8-1 shows several alignment options discussed in this section.

Figure 8-1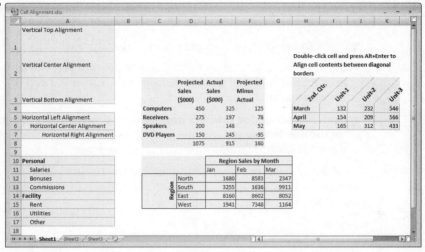

To apply a standard alignment option, select the cell or range that you want to align and then select one of the following options from the Alignment group on the Ribbon's Home tab. (Hover the mouse pointer over an alignment option to display an Extended ScreenTip for the option.)

- ✔ **Vertical alignment:** The options are Top, Center, and Bottom. See cells A1:A3 in Figure 8-1.

- ✔ **Horizontal alignment:** The options are Left, Center, and Right. See cells A5:A7 in Figure 8-1.

- ✔ **Indent:** The options are Increase Indent and Decrease Indent. Multiple clicks on the Increase Indent or Decrease Indent buttons increases or decreases the indent further. See cells A10:A17 in Figure 8-1.

- ✔ **Orientation:** Click the Orientation button to display a menu of predefined orientations. Excel adjusts the row height to display the text. If you don't want this adjustment, you can use the Merge feature first (described shortly) to avoid a larger row height across the worksheet. See cells H3:K3 in Figure 8-1.

- ✔ **Wrap Text:** Select this option when you want a long text entry to take up less horizontal area on the worksheet. See cells D3:F3 in Figure 8-1.

- ✔ **Merge and Center:** You can merge multiple cells into a single, larger cell. This feature enables you to have cells of unequal sizes. If you have a table that spans six columns, for example, you can merge six cells at the top to form a single larger cell for the table's title. In Figure 8-1, cells E10:G10 are merged horizontally, and cells C12:C15 are merged vertically. Note the following rules when merging cells:

- You can merge cells horizontally or vertically.

- If a selection contains more than one nonempty cell, the merged cells contain the contents and formatting of the upper-left cell of the merged range.

- Understanding that *cells* are merged — not the *contents* of cells — is important. Whenever you merge cells, you receive a warning if the selected range contains more than one nonempty cell.

If you do not want to center your data when you merge cells, or if you want to unmerge cells, click the arrow on the Merge and Center button and then choose the appropriate option on the menu.

Changing the Appearance of Cell Contents

By default, Excel formats the information you enter into a worksheet by using the 11-point Calibri font. However, if you want to emphasize various parts of your worksheet, such as the headers in a list, you can apply a different font style, size, color, background, or attribute to the header cells.

To apply a standard formatting option, select the cell or range that you want to format and then select one of the following options from the Format group on the Ribbon's Home tab:

 ✔ **Font Face:** Select a font face from the font picker drop-down list. To preview the change in the selected cell or range before you commit to the change, hover the mouse pointer over a font face in the list.

 ✔ **Font Size:** Select a font size from the font picker drop-down list. To preview the change in the selected cell or range before you commit to the change, hover the mouse pointer over a font size in the list.

 ✔ **Increase/Decrease Font Size:** These buttons increase or decrease the font in the selected cell or range by 2 points.

✔ **Font Style:** The options are Bold, Italic and Underline. Click the arrow on the Underline button if you want to apply a double-underline to the contents of your selected cell or range.

You can also use the following shortcut keys to apply a standard font style to your selection: Ctrl+B for bold, Ctrl+I for italic, and Ctrl+U for underline.

Remember: The Ribbon buttons and shortcut keys act as toggles. You can turn bold on and off, for example, by repeatedly pressing Ctrl+B (or clicking the Bold button).

✔ **Font Color:** Click the Font Color button to apply the color that the button displays to the font in your selected cell or range. Click the arrow on the button to choose a color from the color palette.

✔ **Background Color:** Click the Background Color button to apply the cell background color that the button displays. Click the arrow on the button to select a color from the color palette.

Remember: If you choose non-theme fonts or colors, the fonts or colors don't change if you change the workbook theme. *See also* "Formatting with Themes," in Part 1 and "Using Cell Styles," later in this part.

Copying Formats

The quickest way to copy the formats from one cell to another cell or range is to use the Format Painter button in the Ribbon's Home tab. Follow these steps:

1. Select the cell or range with the formatting attributes that you want to copy.

2. Click the Format Painter button. Notice that the mouse pointer appears as a miniature paintbrush.

3. Select (paint) the cells to which you want to apply the formats.

4. Release the mouse button, and Excel copies the formats.

Double-clicking the Format Painter button causes the mouse pointer to remain a paintbrush after you release the mouse button. This paintbrush enables you to paint other areas of the worksheet with the same formats. To exit paint mode, click the Format Painter button again (or press Esc).

Formatting Based on the Contents of a Cell or Range

In addition to applying static formatting to your worksheet cells and ranges, you can format a cell or range based on the contents of the cell or range. Using Excel *conditional formatting* feature, you can format one or more cells based on the values in the cells, or you can format a range based on the relative values of the cells in the range. You may, for example, want to visually identify all cells in a range that exceed a certain value or you may want to highlight cells in a range having duplicate values.

You can apply any combination of the following standard formatting options when the criteria for formatting the cell are met: Number, Font, Border, and Fill. *See also* "Changing the Appearance of Cell Contents," earlier in this part.

Formatting based on individual cell values

Excel provides several criteria that you can use to format individual cells. Earlier versions of Excel allowed you to format cells based on

- ✔ The value in the cell.

- ✔ A formula. The formula must return a value of True or False for the condition to be applied. For example, to apply a format to cell C3 if the sum of the values in cells A1 to A10 is greater than 2500, you will enter the following conditional formula for cell C3:

  `=SUM($A$1:$A$10)>2500`

  The formula returns True if the sum of cells A1 to A10 is greater than 2500 and False otherwise.

In Excel 2007, you can also format cells based on

- ✔ The cells containing, not containing, beginning with, or ending with specific text. In a list of parts, for example, you can highlight part numbers that contain certain characters.

- ✔ The cells containing dates that match dynamic conditions such as yesterday, today, tomorrow, in the last 7 days, last week, this week, next week, last month, this month, or next month. Excel calculates the date based on your PC's internal real-time clock, so you do not have to update the condition manually.

- ✔ The cells being blank or not blank.

- ✔ The cells having or not having errors.

Follow these steps to conditionally format individual cells or a range of cells:

1. Select the cell or range that you want to format conditionally.

2. Click the Conditional Formatting button on the Ribbon's Home tab. Excel displays a menu of conditional formatting options.

3. Choose Highlight Cells Rules and then choose any option except Duplicate Values from the flyout menu. For example, to format a cell or range of cells if the values in the cells exceed a certain value, choose Greater Than from the flyout menu.

4. In the dialog box that appears (see Figure 8-2), enter a value (or values in the case of Between) in the box on the left. (The label for this box changes depending on what you chose in Step 3.) Instead of entering a value in the Format Cells That Are box, you can click the mouse pointer in the box and point to a cell on the worksheet.

Figure 8-2

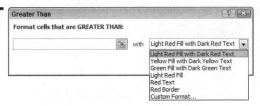

5. If you see a formatting option you like in the drop-down list on the right of the box in which you entered a value, select the option and then click OK to apply the conditional format.

6. If you don't like any of the available formatting options:

   a. Select Custom Format at the bottom of the drop-down list. Excel displays the Format Cells dialog box.

   b. Select your formatting options on the Number, Font, Border, and Fill tabs as appropriate.

   c. Click OK to close the Format Cells dialog box, and then click OK again to apply the conditional format.

Remember: If the cell doesn't meet the condition that you specify, it takes on the standard formatting for the cell.

If you copy a cell containing conditional formatting, the conditional formatting applies to all copies.

Formatting based on values in a range

Excel 2007 provides several criteria that you can use to format cells based on a comparison of the cell values in a range. You can format cells in a range based on

- Duplicate or unique values

- Top *N* items (values), where *N* is a number you specify

- Top *N*% rank, where *N* is a number you specify

- Bottom *N* items (values), where *N* is a number you specify

- Bottom *N*% rank, where *N* is a number you specify

- Above average values

- Below average values

- Average or above average values

- Average or below average values

   ✔ One to three standard deviations above average values

   ✔ One to three standard deviations below average values

Follow these steps to conditionally format a range of cells based on a comparison of the cells in the range:

1. Select the range that you want to format conditionally.

2. Click the Conditional Formatting button on the Ribbon's Home tab. Excel displays a menu of conditional formatting options.

3. Choose one of the following options:

    • To highlight duplicate or unique values in the range, choose Highlight Cells Rules and then choose Duplicate Values from the flyout menu.

    • To highlight the top *N* value cells, top *N*% rank cells, and so on, choose Top/Bottom Rules and then choose an option in the flyout menu.

4. In the dialog box that appears (see Figure 8-3 for an example), select the value option on the left side and a formatting option on the right side drop-down list.

Figure 8-3

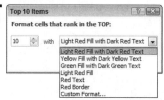

5. If you see a formatting option you like in the drop-down list, select the option and click OK to apply the conditional format.

6. If you don't like any of the available formatting options:

    a. Select Custom Format at the bottom of the list. Excel displays the Format Cells dialog box.

    b. Choose your formatting options on the Number, Font, Border, and Fill tabs as appropriate.

    c. Click OK to close the Format Cells dialog box, and then click OK again to apply the conditional format.

Applying multiple conditional formats to a cell or range

Excel allows you to specify more than one conditional format for a cell. For example, you can have different formatting for a cell based on the value in the cell.

In earlier versions of Excel, you were limited to a maximum of three conditional formats per cell. In Excel 2007, the number of conditional formats per cell is limited only by your PC's memory. Also, Excel 2007 allows you to apply multiple conditional formats to a cell if more than one condition is True. For example, if one conditional format applies a bold font when a formatting condition is True, and another makes the cell background color red when a second formatting condition is True, Excel applies both formats to the cell if the two conditions evaluate to True. If the formatting conflicts (for example a red font and a green font), Excel applies only the first rule that meets the condition.

Follow these steps to add an additional conditional format for a cell or range:

1. Select the cell or range that already contains one conditional format.

2. Click the Conditional Formatting button on the Ribbon's Home tab and choose Manage Rules (at the bottom of the menu). Excel displays the Conditional Formatting Rules Manager dialog box, as shown in Figure 8-4.

Figure 8-4

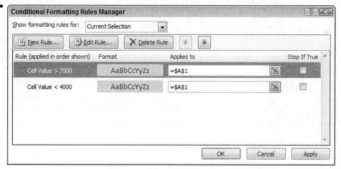

The Conditional Formatting Rules Manager dialog box is new in Excel 2007. By default, the window displays the conditional formatting rule(s) applied to the current selection. If you weren't sure of the range in Step 1, you can click the Show Formatting Rules For drop-down list and select This Worksheet (or other worksheets in the workbook). The rules window then displays all the conditional formatting rules and the ranges to which the rule(s) apply. Make note of the range to which you want to add a new rule, exit the dialog box, and begin again at Step 1.

3. In the dialog box, click the New rule button. Excel displays the New Formatting Rule dialog box.

4. In the Select a Rule Type list, choose a rule type. To apply standard conditional formatting options (number, font, border or patterns), do *not* select the first option in the window (Format All Cells Based on Their Values). The controls that appear initially in the Edit the Rules Description section depend on the rule type you chose.

5. In the leftmost drop-down list in the Edit the Rules Description section, choose an option (for all choices in Step 4 except Use a Formula to Determine Which Cells to Format). New controls appear to the right of this drop-down list depending on your choice. Complete the requirements for the controls (for example, enter a value, enter a cell reference, or choose from a list).

6. Click Format to display the Format Cells dialog box and select your formatting options from among the available tabs.

7. Click OK to exit the dialog box, and click OK again to exit the New Formatting Rule dialog box. Excel returns you to the Conditional Formatting Rules Manager dialog box.

8. Excel evaluates conditional formatting rules in the order listed in the Conditional Formatting Rules Manager dialog box. To change the evaluation order of a rule, select the rule and click the up or down arrow to the right of the Delete rule button.

9. Click OK.

Editing or deleting a conditional format

Follow these steps if you want to edit a condition for a cell or range or delete a condition for a cell or range with multiple conditions:

1. Select the cell or range that contains the conditional format you want to edit or delete.

2. Click the Conditional Formatting button on the Ribbon's Home tab, and then choose Manage Rules (at the bottom of the menu). Excel displays the Conditional Formatting Rules Manager dialog box.

3. In the Conditional Formatting Rules Manager dialog box, select the condition you want to edit or delete.

4. Do one of the following:

   • To delete the condition, click Delete.

   • To edit the condition, click Edit. Make your changes in the Edit Formatting Rule dialog box that appears and then click OK.

5. Click OK.

 To quickly delete (clear) all conditional formatting rules for a cell or range, select the cell or range, click the Conditional Formatting button on the Ribbon's home tab, choose Clear Rules from the menu, and then choose Selected Cells from the flyout menu. To quickly delete (clear) all conditional formatting rules for the active worksheet, choose Entire Sheet from the Clear Rules flyout menu.

Formatting Numbers

Excel internally stores all numbers and dates that you enter in your worksheet as plain, unformatted numbers. You can use Excel's built-in numeric and date/time formats to make your data more readable and understandable. In addition, if you can't find a suitable built-in format to fit your needs, you can create a custom number format.

Using Excel's built-in number formats

Excel is smart enough to perform some number formatting for you automatically. If you enter **9.6%** into a cell, for example, Excel knows that you want to use a percentage format and applies it for you automatically. Similarly, if you use commas to separate thousands (such as **123,456**) or a dollar sign to indicate currency (such as **$123.45**), Excel applies the appropriate formatting for you.

Use the buttons in the Number group of the Ribbon's Home tab to quickly apply common number formats. After you click one of these buttons, the active cell takes on the specified number format.

 You can select among several currency symbols by clicking the arrow on the Accounting Number Format button in the Number group of the Ribbon's Home tab and choosing a symbol from the menu.

To access additional number formats, click the arrow on the Number Format drop-down list above the number format buttons and select an option from the list.

If none of the predefined number format buttons or Number Format list options fit the bill, you need to use the Format Cells dialog box. Follow these steps to select an option from the Format Cells dialog box:

1. Select a cell or range of cells you want to format.

2. Click the arrow on the Number Format drop-down list and select More Number Formats at the bottom of the list; or click the Number dialog launcher button at the bottom right of the Number group container. Excel displays the Format Cells dialog box with the Number tab selected.

3. In the Category list box, select one of the categories. After you choose a category, the right side of the dialog box changes to display the appropriate options.

4. Choose an option from the right side of the dialog box. The top of the dialog box displays a sample of how the active cell appears with the number format you chose.

5. Click OK to apply the number format to all the selected cells.

Remember: If the cell displays a series of pound signs (such as ####), it means the column isn't wide enough to display the value using the number format you chose. The solution is to make the column wider or to change the number format. ***See*** "Changing column width," later in this part.

Creating custom number formats

Excel provides many predefined number formats, but if none of these formats are satisfactory, you need to create a custom number format. Just follow these steps:

1. Complete Steps 1 to 3 for accessing the Format Cells dialog box as detailed in the preceding section, but in Step 3, select Custom in the Category list box.

2. Construct a number format by selecting an option from the right list box or by specifying a series of codes in the Type text box (located above the list box). In the Type text box, you can also modify a code you select from the list box. The Sample area shows how an entry in the active cell will be displayed with the code specified in the Type text box.

3. Click OK to store the custom number format and apply it to the selected cells. The custom number format is now available for you to use with other cells in the workbook.

To find out more about the meaning of custom formatting codes, check out this online resource:

http://office.microsoft.com/en-us/assistance/HP051986791033.aspx

After reviewing the online information, it will become clearer how Excel constructs its built-in number formats. Click a cell with a built-in format, and then display the Format Cells dialog box as already described and select the custom option in the Category list box. The text box on the right of the dialog box displays the formatting code for the built-in format. If you want, you can create a custom format by modifying a built-in format.

Remember: Excel stores custom number formats with the workbook. To make the custom format available in a different workbook, you must copy a cell that uses the custom format to the other workbook.

Formatting Ranges Using Visualizations

Visualizations allow you to compare the relative values in a range visually. Excel 2007 uses special conditional formatting within the cells to make this relative comparison. Visual comparisons are particularly useful if you have a lot of data to analyze, because you can quickly detect trends, spot outliers (a value far from most others in a data set), compare performance (good, bad, or neutral) and so on. Excel 2007 provides the following three special conditional formatting tools for comparing the relative values in a range:

- ✔ **Data bar:** Uses horizontal bars to compare the relative sizes of values in the range.

- ✔ **Color scale:** Uses color gradients (such as various shades of red, amber, and green) to compare the variation of values in the range.

- ✔ **Icon set:** Uses a set of icons (for example up, down, and horizontal arrows) to compare values in the range.

Figure 8-5 shows examples of each visualization type.

Figure 8-5

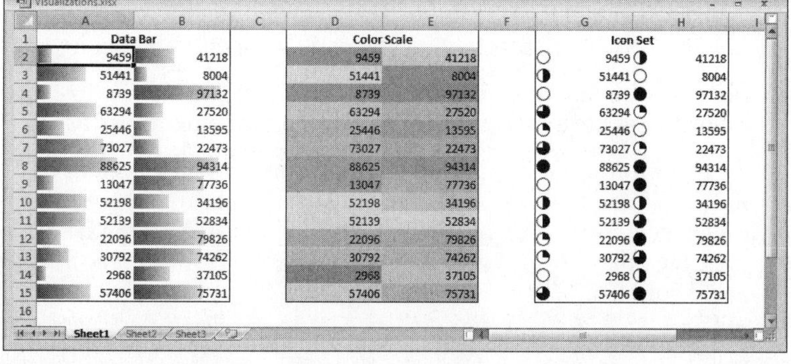

Using a visualization to compare values in a range

To use a visualization to compare relative values in a range, follow these steps:

1. Select the range.

2. Click the Conditional Formatting button on the Ribbon's Home tab. Excel displays a menu of conditional formatting options.

3. Choose one of the following options from the menu:

- Data Bars. Choose a bar color from the flyout menu. By default, Excel uses the highest and lowest values in the range to draw the longest and shortest bar, respectively. To allow the shortest bar to show in a cell when there is a wide variation between the smallest and largest value in the range, Excel sets the shortest bar to ten percent of the cell width.

- Color Scales. Choose a color scale from the flyout menu. By default, Excel uses the lowest, highest, and midpoint values in the range to determine the color gradients.

- Icon Sets. Choose an icon set from the flyout menu. You can choose icon sets having three, four, or five icons. By default, Excel uses percentages to determine the break between icons. In the case of a three-icon set, for example, Excel sets 33% and 67% as the break between the three icons.

If you hover the mouse pointer over an option in any flyout menu, Excel shows a preview of the visualization that will be applied to the range.

Modifying the visualization for a range

After you create a visualization for a range, you can modify the visualization in several ways. You can use a different visualization, change the type of comparison among the values in the range, or display the visualization without the cell values.

Follow these steps to modify the visualization for a range:

1. Select the range that contains the visualization you want to edit.

2. Click the Conditional Formatting button on the Ribbon's Home tab and then choose Manage Rules (at the bottom of the menu). Excel displays the Conditional Formatting Rules Manager dialog box.

3. In the Conditional Formatting Rules Manager dialog box, click the Edit rule button. If you have more than one conditional formatting rule applied to a range, select the rule you want to modify in the window before clicking the Edit rule button. Excel displays the Edit Formatting Rule dialog box. See Figure 8-6.

4. In the Select a Rule Type list, ensure that Format All Cells Based on Their Values is selected.

Figure 8-6

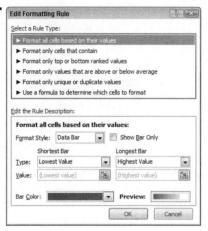

5. In the Edit the Rule Description section, select your options:

- If you want to change the visualization in the selected range, select a new option in the Format Style drop-down list.

- If you want a different comparison for the relative values in the range, first make a selection from the Type drop-down list. The options are Lowest or Highest value (applicable to data bars and color scales), Number, Percent, Percentile, and Formula.

  Next, enter values for the type of comparison you chose. The Value option is not available if you choose Lowest Value or Highest Value for the comparison type. The values you enter have different meaning for the visualization you choose: For data bars, the values and comparison type combine to determine the bar size for each value in the selected range. For color scales, the values and comparison type combine to determine the color assigned to each value in the selected range. for icon sets, the values and comparison type combine to determine the icon assigned to each value in the selected range.

- To choose a different bar color for a data bar, different colors for the lowest, highest, and midpoint (if applicable) values for a color scale, or a different icon set style for a displayed icon set, make a selection in the Bar Color or Icon Style drop-down list.

- If you want to display data bars or icons in the selected range without the associated values, select the Show Bar or Icon Only check box (available after you choose a data bar or icon set format style, respectively).

6. Click Preview to preview the changes in the selected range and then click OK to apply the changes.

Hiding Cell Contents

You can hide the contents of a cell by using either of the following formatting options:

- ✔ Apply a custom number format consisting of three semicolons (; ; ;). **See** "Creating custom number formats," earlier in this part.

- ✔ Make the text color the same as the background color. **See** "Changing the Appearance of Cell Contents," earlier in this part.

Both formatting techniques have the same flaw: If the active cell pointer is on the cell, its contents are visible in the formula bar. To avoid this flaw and make the cell contents truly invisible, you should protect the worksheet after you choose one of the preceding options. **See also** "Protecting a Worksheet," in Part 3.

Hiding and Unhiding Columns and Rows

Hiding columns and rows is useful if you don't want users to see particular information or if you don't want some information to print. Alternatively, you can unhide rows or columns to reveal information.

Hiding columns and rows

To hide a column(s) or row(s), choose one of the following options:

- ✔ Select any cell(s) on the worksheet in the column(s) or row(s) that you want to hide. In the Ribbon's Home tab, choose Format⇨Hide & Unhide⇨Hide Columns; or Format⇨Hide & Unhide⇨Hide Rows.

- ✔ Select the column or row header(s) you want to hide. **See** "Selecting entire rows and columns," in Part 4. In the Ribbon's Home tab, choose Format⇨ Hide & Unhide⇨Hide Columns; or Format⇨Hide & Unhide⇨Hide Rows; or right-click the selected row or column header(s) and choose Hide from the contextual menu.

- ✔ Drag a column header's right border all the way to the left or a row header's bottom border all the way upward.

Remember: A hidden column or row has a width or height of 0. If you use the arrow keys to move the active cell pointer, you skip cells in hidden columns or rows. In other words, you can't use the arrow keys to move to a cell in a hidden row or column.

See also the next section, "Unhiding columns and rows."

Unhiding columns and rows

Unhiding a hidden row or column can prove a bit tricky because you can't directly select a row or column that's hidden.

To unhide a column(s) or row(s), choose one of the following options:

✔ Select any cells on the worksheets on either side of the column(s) or row(s) that you want to unhide. In Figure 8-7, for example, if you want to unhide columns E and F, select any row on the worksheet and select cells in columns D and G. In the Ribbon's Home tab, choose Format➪Hide & Unhide➪Unhide Columns; or Format➪Hide & Unhide➪Unhide Rows.

Figure 8-7

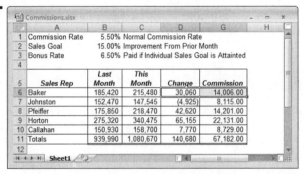

	A	B	C	D	G	H
1	Commission Rate	5.50%	Normal Commission Rate			
2	Sales Goal	15.00%	Improvement From Prior Month			
3	Bonus Rate	6.50%	Paid if Individual Sales Goal is Attainted			
4						
5	**Sales Rep**	*Last Month*	*This Month*	*Change*	*Commission*	
6	Baker	185,420	215,480	30,060	14,006.00	
7	Johnston	152,470	147,545	(4,925)	8,115.00	
8	Pfeiffer	175,850	218,470	42,620	14,201.00	
9	Horton	275,320	340,475	65,155	22,131.00	
10	Callahan	150,930	158,700	7,770	8,729.00	
11	Totals	939,990	1,080,670	140,680	67,182.00	
12						

Commissions.xlsx — Sheet1

✔ Select the column or row header(s) on either side of the row(s) or column(s) you want to unhide. ***See*** "Selecting entire rows and columns," in Part 4. In the Ribbon's Home tab, choose Format➪Hide & Unhide➪Unhide Columns; or Format➪Hide & Unhide➪Unhide Rows; or right-click the selected row or column header(s) and choose Unhide from the contextual menu.

TIP
To unhide all hidden columns or rows, select the entire worksheet (by pressing Ctrl+A or clicking the blank box that intersects the row and column headings) and then choose Format➪Hide & Unhide➪Unhide Columns; or Format➪Hide & Unhide➪Unhide Rows

Modifying Cell Size

You may want to change the width of a column if it's not wide enough to display values (indicated when the column displays a series of pound signs — ######) or to simply space out the cells horizontally. Changing the row height is useful for spacing out rows and is sometimes better than inserting empty rows between rows of data.

Changing column width

To change the width of a column(s), choose one of the following options:

✔ Select any cell(s) on the worksheets in the column(s) that you want to adjust. On the Ribbon's Home tab, click the Format button, choose Width from the menu, and enter a value in the Column Width dialog box that appears. Alternatively, choose AutoFit Selection from the menu. This command adjusts the width of the selected column(s) so that the widest entry in the column fits.

✔ Drag the right border of the column heading with the mouse until the column is the width that you want. As you drag, Excel displays a ScreenTip that shows the current column width (see Figure 8-8). If you select multiple column headers and drag the right border of any one of the column headers, all columns adjust accordingly.

Figure 8-8

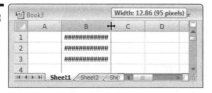

✔ Double-click the right border of a column heading to automatically set the column width to the widest entry in the column. If you select multiple column headers and double-click the right border of any one of the column headers, each column width is set automatically to the widest entry in the column.

✔ Select the column heading(s) of the column(s) you want to adjust. Right-click the column header(s), choose Column Width from the contextual menu, and enter a value in the Column Width dialog box that appears.

TIP To change the default width of all columns, click the Format button and choose Standard Width from the menu. This command opens the Standard Width dialog box, in which you enter the new default column width. All columns that weren't previously adjusted take on the new column width.

Changing row height

You measure row height in *points* (a standard unit of measurement in the printing trade; 72 points equal 1 inch). To change the height of a row(s), choose one of the following options:

✔ Select any cell(s) on the worksheets in the row(s) that you want to adjust. On the Ribbon's Home tab, click the Format button, choose Height from the menu, and enter a value in the Row Height dialog box that appears.

✔ Drag the bottom border of the row heading with the mouse until the row is the height that you want. As you drag, Excel displays a ScreenTip that shows the current row height. If you select multiple row headers and drag the bottom border of any one of the row headers, all rows adjust accordingly.

✔ Select the row heading(s) of the row(s) you want to adjust. Right-click the row header(s), choose Row Height from the contextual menu, and enter a value in the Row Height dialog box that appears.

Remember: Excel adjusts the row height automatically to accommodate the tallest entry in the row.

Using Cell Styles

If you find yourself continuously applying the same combination of fonts, lines, shading, number format, and so on to cells or ranges in your worksheet, using cell styles instead will save you time.

Excel 2007 provides a Cell Styles gallery with several predefined styles (see Figure 8-9.) You can modify a predefined style or create a new style from scratch. The Cell Styles gallery includes Titles and Heading styles and Themed Cell styles categories that change if you change the workbook theme. The default font used for styles in the other predefined categories in the gallery matches the body font of the selected theme and therefore changes as the theme changes. *See also* "Formatting with Themes," in Part 1.

Figure 8-9

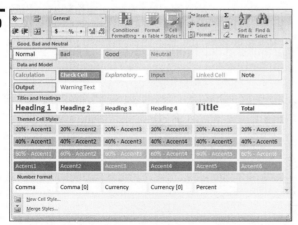

A cell style can include any combination of the following formatting elements:

- Number format
- Font (type, size, and color)
- Alignment (vertical and horizontal)
- Border
- Pattern
- Protection (locked and hidden)

Applying a predefined cell style

Follow these steps to apply a predefined style:

1. Select the cell or range to which you want to apply the style. You can select a contiguous or noncontiguous range. **See also** "Selecting Cells and Ranges," in Part 4.

2. Click the Cell Styles button on the Ribbon's Home tab. Excel displays a gallery of predefined styles.

3. Choose a style from the gallery to immediately apply the style. If you hover the mouse pointer over a style, Excel provides a preview of the style in your selected cell or range. The style is not applied until you actually select (click) it.

The Cells Styles gallery includes a few categories with styles that you can use as a guide for representing certain types of data. For example, you can use the Good, Bad, and Neutral styles to highlight data in your worksheet that's considered good, bad, or neutral. You can use the Data and Model styles to represent input cells, cells that involve calculations (formulas), and so on. These two style categories use a theme font and non-theme colors. If you select a new theme for the workbook, the font changes to match the new theme but the colors remain unchanged.

Select a style from the Themed Cell style category if you want to format a range to match other elements on the worksheet that use theme styles (a chart, for example). If you change the theme applied to the workbook, the formatting of the range changes to match the new theme.

See also "Formatting with Themes," in Part 1.

Modifying an existing style

The Cell Styles gallery is an example of the Ribbon's *results-oriented* approach. The Cell Styles gallery provides predefined layouts that you're likely to be satisfied with. However, if none of the available styles are exactly what you want but are close, you can simply modify an existing style rather than create a new style from scratch. For example, you might be happy with a certain style's font and background color but not the number format, or you might like the number format and font but not the background color.

Follow these steps to modify an existing style:

1. Click the Cell Styles button on the Ribbon's Home tab, right-click a style, and choose Modify from the menu that appears. Excel displays the Style dialog box.

2. If you want, type a new name for the style in the Style Name box.

3. In the Style Includes section, click to add or clear a check mark next to the formatting elements you want to include or not include in the modified style.

4. Click the Format button. Excel displays the Format Cells dialog box.

5. Select the appropriate tabs and formatting options you want.

6. Click OK to exit the Format Cells dialog box and click OK again to close the Style dialog box. Excel updates the style in the gallery with the changes you made.

Creating a custom cell style

If none of the styles available in the Cell Styles gallery meet your needs either directly or by modifying a style, you can create a style from scratch. Follow these steps to create a custom cell style:

1. Click the Cell Styles button on the Ribbon's Home tab, and then choose New Cell Style (at the bottom of the gallery). Excel displays the Style dialog box.

2. In the Style Name box, type a name for the style.

3. Complete Steps 3 to 6 in the section "Modifying an existing style," immediately preceding this section. Excel adds the style to a new Custom category section it creates in the Cell Styles gallery.

Copying (merging) cell styles from another workbook

If you modify existing styles or create several custom styles in a workbook, you may want these styles to appear in other workbooks. Merging styles from another workbook can save a lot of time because you don't have to recreate the styles manually in every new workbook in which you want to use the styles.

Follow these steps to merge a style from another workbook:

1. Ensure that the workbook from which you want to merge the styles is open.

2. Activate the workbook you want to merge the styles to.

3. Click the Cell Styles button on the Ribbon's Home tab, and then choose Merge Styles (at the bottom of the gallery). Excel displays the Merge Styles dialog box.

4. In the Merge Styles From list box, select the workbook from which you will be merging the styles and click OK.

5. Excel asks you to confirm whether you want to merge styles with the same names as styles in the workbook that you're merging to. In most cases, you want to click No. Excel merges the styles into the active workbook.

6. To view the merged styles, click the Cell Styles button.

Part 9

Printing Your Work

Many worksheets that you develop with Excel are designed to serve as printed reports. Printing from Excel is easy, and you can generate attractive reports with minimal effort. Excel offers numerous printing options, which we explain in this part.

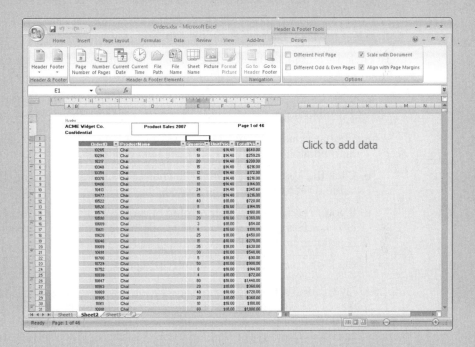

In this part . . .

- ✏ **Changing the Worksheet Display Mode**
- ✏ **Controlling Page Settings**
- ✏ **Handling Page Breaks**
- ✏ **Inserting a Header or Footer**
- ✏ **Setting Sheet Printing Options**
- ✏ **Specifying What You Want to Print**

Adjusting Margins and Centering Printed Output

Margins are the blank spaces that border a printed page (top, bottom, left, and right). The wider the margins, the less space that is available for printing. You can control all four page margins from Excel.

To adjust the margins, follow these steps:

1. Click the Page Layout View button on the status bar or in the Ribbon's View tab. Although you can set margins in normal display mode, you will see exactly how the margin settings will affect your printout in page layout view.

2. Select the Page Layout tab on the Ribbon.

3. Click the Margins button, and choose an option from the gallery. Excel applies the new margin settings to your worksheet.

4. If you need finer control over the margin settings, or if you want to center your printed output

   a. Choose Custom Margins from the gallery. Excel displays the Page Setup dialog box with the Margins tab selected.

   b. Click the appropriate spinner to change the margin value (or enter a value directly in one of the boxes).

   c. If you need to center your printed output, select one or both of the check boxes (Vertical and Horizontal) in the Center on Page section of the dialog box.

   d. Click OK to close the Page Setup dialog box.

Another way to adjust the margins in page layout view is through the rulers. The rulers appear at the top and the left of the page containing the active cell pointer. The document print area is within the white portion of the rulers. The margins are represented by the dark areas on the rulers (which border the print area). To adjust the margins, drag the boundary between the print and margin areas (left, right, top, and bottom). After you place the mouse pointer on a margin boundary, the pointer changes to a horizontal double-headed arrow and Excel display a ScreenTip indicating the margin name (Left, Right, Top, or Bottom) and the margin size.

Remember: You can turn the rulers on or off by selecting the Ruler option on the Ribbon's View tab.

Changing Default Print Settings Using a Template

If you find that you're never satisfied with the Excel default print settings, you may want to create a template with the print settings you use most often. To create such a template, follow these steps:

1. Start with an empty workbook. *See* "Creating an Empty Workbook File," in Part 2.

2. Adjust the print settings to your liking. Use the appropriate section in this part if you need assistance with a particular setting.

3. Save the workbook as a template in your xlstart folder, using the name **Book.xlt**. *See* "Creating a default workbook template," in Part 2.

Excel uses this template as the basis for all new workbooks, and your custom print settings become the default settings.

Changing the Worksheet Display Mode

Excel provides the following two special display modes that you can work in with documents you intend to print:

✔ **Page break preview:** This display mode shows a birds-eye view of your worksheet with lines indicating the location of page breaks and page number watermarks identifying the pages. This display mode is useful for setting or adjusting page breaks.

✔ **Page layout view:** The new page layout view shows your work in the context of the printed page (see Figure 9-1). This display mode has the following characteristics:

- Shows individual pages with headers and footers, margins, page orientation, and common worksheet print settings (such as row and column headers or row and column data labels if selected.)

- The view is fully editable, so that you can use this mode in lieu of the normal display mode for any document you intend to print. Note, however, that you will see less data on-screen than in Normal display mode.

- The pages that will not print are shaded and contain the phrase *Click to add data* watermark.

Left margin area

Top
margin   Left header area
area   Right header area
                        Ruler   Center header area
                                                              Right margin area

Figure 9-1

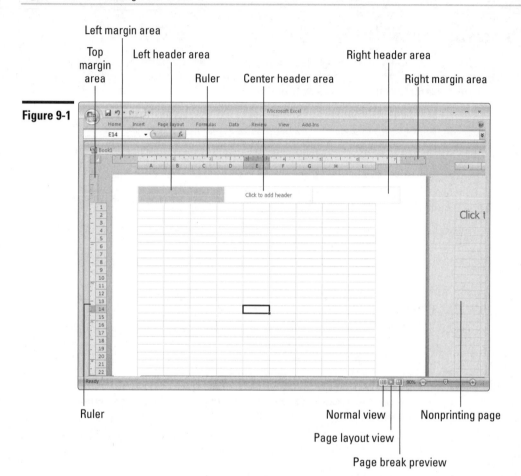

Ruler   Normal view   Nonprinting page

                                                   Page layout view

                                                   Page break preview

You can switch between display modes easily by clicking a display mode button
on the right side of the status bar (see Figure 9-1) or by clicking a mode button
in the Ribbon's View tab.

Controlling Page Settings

You can control how a page prints using several options, including orientation,
paper size, and scaling. This section describes how to use the more common
page options.

Changing page orientation

To change the page orientation (to landscape or portrait) of your printed output, click the Page Layout tab on the Ribbon, click the Orientation button, and choose either the Portrait or Landscape option from the menu.

Selecting paper size

To change the paper size of the printed output, click the Page Layout tab on the Ribbon, click the Size button, and choose a size from the menu.

Scaling your printed output

The data in a worksheet can span across several columns and down several rows. Sometimes, you may want to set the number of pages that your data spans across and down so that you can view more or less data on the printed page. Alternatively, you may want to scale the printed output to a higher or lower percentage of the actual size. To scale your printed output, follow these steps:

1. Click the Page Layout tab on the Ribbon.

2. Do one (or more) of the following:

- To scale the width of the printout to fit within a set number of pages, choose the number of pages from the Width drop-down list.

- To scale the height of the printout to fit within a set number of pages, choose the number of pages from the Height drop-down list.

- To scale the printed output to a higher or lower percentage of actual size, use the Scale spinner arrows to set the percentage or enter a percentage value in the spinner box. For this feature to work, you must set the Width and Height options to automatic.

Specifying the beginning page number

If you intend to insert your printed output into another report, you may want to specify a beginning page number so that the pages collate correctly as you insert them into the report. To do so, follow these steps:

1. Select the Page Layout tab on the Ribbon and click the dialog launcher button at the bottom right of the Page Setup group container. Excel displays the Page dialog box with the Page tab selected.

2. Specify a page number for the first page in the First Page Number text box. The default option is set to Auto, which starts numbering at page 1.

3. Click OK to close the Page Setup dialog box.

Handling Page Breaks

If you print multiple-page reports, you know that controlling page breaks is often important. You normally don't want a row to print on a page by itself, for example. Excel handles page breaks automatically. After you print or preview your worksheet, Excel displays dashed lines on the worksheet in normal display mode to indicate where page breaks occur. Sometimes, you want to force a page break — either a vertical or a horizontal one. If your worksheet consists of several distinct areas, for example, you may want to print each area on a separate sheet of paper.

Inserting manual page breaks

To override Excel's automatic handling of page breaks, you must manually insert one or more page breaks. To insert a horizontal page break, follow these steps:

1. Move the cell pointer to the row where you want to begin the new page, but make sure that the cell pointer is in column A. (Otherwise, you insert a vertical page break *and* a horizontal page break.)

2. Click the Page Layout tab on the Ribbon, click the Page Break button, and choose Insert Page Break from the menu. Excel inserts the page break in the row that is above the cell pointer.

To insert a vertical page break, follow these steps:

1. Move the cell pointer to the column that you want to begin the new page, but make sure that the cell pointer is in row 1. (Otherwise, you insert a horizontal page break *and* a vertical page break).

2. Click the Page Layout tab on the Ribbon, click the Breaks button, and choose Insert Page Break from the menu. Excel inserts the page break in the column to the left of the cell pointer.

 You can often get a better perspective of where to insert breaks in your worksheet by creating your page breaks in the page break preview display mode. *See* "Previewing and adjusting page breaks," later in this section.

Removing manual page breaks

To remove a manual page break, follow these steps:

1. Move the cell pointer anywhere in the first row *below* a horizontal page break or in the first column to the *right* of a vertical page break.

2. Click the Page Layout tab on the Ribbon, click the Breaks button, and choose Remove Page Break from the menu.

TIP

To remove all manual page breaks in the worksheet, click the Page Layout tab on the Ribbon, click the Breaks button, and choose Reset All Page Breaks from the menu.

Previewing and adjusting page breaks

Click the Page Break Preview button on the right side of the status bar or click the Page Break Preview button on the Ribbon's View tab to enter the page break preview mode. This mode displays your worksheet in a way that enables you to move the page breaks by dragging them with your mouse (see Figure 9-2). This view doesn't show a true page preview. (For example, it doesn't show headers and footers.) But it's an easy way to make sure that the pages break at desired locations.

Figure 9-2

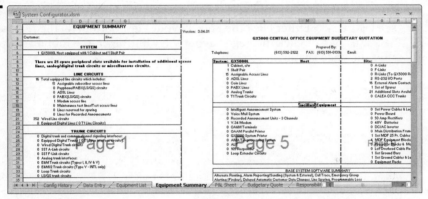

Remember the following points as you use the page break preview mode:

- ✔ Excel automatically zooms out so that you can see more on-screen. You can set the zoom factor to any value that you want by using the zoom controls on the status bar.

- ✔ If you specify a print area (rather than the entire worksheet), the print area appears in white and all the other cells appear in a darker color.

- ✔ You can adjust a page break by dragging the line that identifies a break location.

- ✔ In this display mode, Excel shows manual page breaks as solid lines and automatic breaks as dashed lines.

- ✔ While you're previewing the page breaks, you have full access to all Excel commands.

Remember: If you increase the amount of information to be printed on a page having a manual break, Excel automatically scales the output to fit the page.

Inserting a Header or Footer

A *header* is information that appears at the top of each printed page. A *footer* is information that appears at the bottom of each printed page.

Headers and footers each have three sections: left, center, and right. You can, for example, specify a header that consists of your name left-justified, the worksheet name centered, and the page number right-justified.

 The easiest way to include a header or footer in your printouts is to add the header or footer in the header and footer regions of the page layout view mode (see Figure 9-3). Either click the Page Layout View button, on the right side of the status bar, or click the Page Layout View button on the Ribbon's View tab to enter the page layout view mode.

Figure 9-3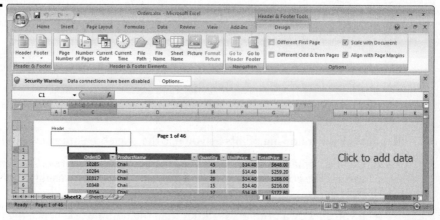

The header and footer regions in the page layout view have the following characteristics:

    ✔ The regions appear immediately above and below the worksheet data area.

    ✔ If the header or footer regions are empty, the center section of each region includes a watermark. The header watermark is labeled *Click to add header* and the footer watermark is labeled *Click to add footer.*

✔ If you hover the mouse pointer over a header or footer section, Excel shades the section to indicate the area that the section covers. Simply click in a section to add information.

✔ By default, the same header and footer appears on each page.

✔ Excel displays the information in the header or footer area as it would appear on the printed page.

Remember: By default, Excel doesn't automatically include a header or footer in your printouts if you don't specify any information to include in the header or footer.

Selecting a predefined header or footer

To select a predefined header or footer, follow these steps:

1. Select the Page Layout View by clicking the Page Layout View button on the status bar or in the Ribbon's View tab.

2. Click in a section of the header or footer region. The Ribbon displays the Header & Footer Tools contextual tab header on Excel's title bar and the Design tab below the header.

3. If necessary, click the Design tab to display the header/footer tools on the Ribbon.

4. Click the Header or Footer button and choose an option from the menu.

5. Click anywhere on the worksheet to remove the display of the header/footer tools on the Ribbon. Excel inserts the selected header or footer on the page.

Remember: You can insert the header/footer information on any page of your document and Excel will automatically apply the header/footer to all other pages. *See also* "Using multiple headers and footers in your reports," later in this section.

Creating a custom header or footer

To define a custom header or footer, follow these steps:

1. Complete Steps 1 to 3 in "Selecting a predefined header or footer," immediately preceding in this section.

2. Enter the desired information in any of or all the three sections of the header or footer; or click any of the eight buttons in the Header and Footer Elements group (described in the following table) to enter a special code.

Button	Code	Function
Page Number	&[Page]	Inserts the page number
Number of Pages	&[Pages]	Inserts the total number of pages to print
Current Date	&[Date]	Inserts the current date
Current Time	&[Time]	Inserts the current time
File Path	&[Path]&[File]	Inserts the path and filename of the workbook
File Name	&[File]	Inserts the workbook's name
Sheet Name	&[Tab]	Inserts the sheet's name
Picture	&[Picture]	Inserts a picture in the header or footer

After you click away from the section in which you added a code, Excel converts the code to the actual information that will appear on the printed page.

3. If you need to format the header or footer text, click the Ribbon's Home tab and select from the available tools in the Font group.

4. Click anywhere on the worksheet to remove the display of the header/footer tools on the Ribbon.

The Format Picture button in the Header and Footer Elements group is available only if you insert a picture in the header or footer. Clicking this button displays the Format Picture dialog box, in which you can select options to size, rotate, scale, crop, and adjust the picture.

You can combine text and codes and insert as many codes as you want into each section. If the text that you enter uses an ampersand (&), you must enter it twice (because Excel uses an ampersand to signal a code). For example, to enter the text *Research & Development* into a header or footer, type *Research && Development.*

You can use as many lines as you want in your header or footer section. You may have to adjust the top or bottom margin, however, to prevent the header or footer from spilling into the worksheet area. Position the mouse pointer where to want to add another line or wrap an existing line, and press Enter.

Remember: You insert the header/footer information on any page of your document and Excel automatically applies the header/footer to all other pages. **See also** "Using multiple headers and footers in your reports," immediately following this section.

Using multiple headers and footers in your reports

Excel 2007 provides the following options when specifying headers and footers for different pages in your reports:

- ✔ You can specify a different header/footer for the first page. This option is useful, for example, for reports that require a different header or footer for a title or table of contents page.

- ✔ You can specify a different header/footer for odd and even pages. This option is useful, for example, if you create book-style reports. If, in addition, you specify a first page header or footer, Excel will apply the odd page header or footer starting from the second page of your report.

Follow these steps to add a separate header/footer to the first page or to add separate headers/footers to odd and even pages of your report:

1. Complete Steps 1 to 3 in "Selecting a predefined header or footer," earlier in this section.

2. Do one or both of the following:

    - To specify a first page header/footer, select the Different First Page check box in the Options group of the Header and Footer Design tab.

    - To specify odd and even page headers/footers, select the Different Odd & Even Pages check box in the Options group of the Header and Footer Design tab.

3. Enter the header or footer information for each page as follows:

    - If you specified a separate first page header/footer only, enter the first page header/footer information in the first page of your document and enter the header/footer information for all subsequent pages in the second page of your document.

    - If you specified odd and even headers/footers only, enter the header/footer information for all odd pages in the first page of your document and enter the header/footer information for all even pages in the second page of your document.

    - If you specified both first page header/footer and odd and even page headers/footers, enter the first page header/footer information in the first page of your document, enter the header/footer information for all odd pages in the second page of your document, and enter the header/footer information for all even pages in the third page of your document.

Remember: When you click the mouse pointer within a header or footer region, Excel indicates the type of header/footer you're working with (normal, first page, odd page, or even page) above the header or below the footer area.

Previewing Your Work

The Excel print preview feature shows an image of the printed output on your screen — a handy feature that saves time and paper.

To access the print preview feature, click the Office button, then click the arrow on the Print option in the menu and choose Print Preview from the right side of the menu.

Remember: If you work in the page layout view, you will see some but not all print options — for example, you won't see the print gridlines, print draft quality, print black and white, and print error display options. You must use the print preview feature to preview *all* your selected print options.

Remember: Unlike the other display modes discussed in this part, you can't work in print preview. You can't enter or edit data, format your data, adjust page breaks, create charts and so on.

Printing with Quick Print

Quick Print allows you to print the current worksheet using the default print settings. If you changed any of the default print settings, Excel uses the settings that you entered; otherwise, it uses the following default settings:

- Prints the active worksheet (or all selected worksheets), including any embedded charts or drawing objects
- Prints one copy
- Prints in portrait mode
- Does not scale the printed output
- Uses 0.75-inch top and bottom margins and 0.7-inch left and right margins
- Does not print a header or footer
- For wide worksheets that span multiple pages, prints down and then over
- Prints to the default printer

To print without changing default settings, click the Office button, click the arrow at the end of the Print option, and choose Quick Print from the flyout menu.

 You can add a button to the Quick Access toolbar that allows you to print with a single mouse click. Simply click the arrow to the right of the Quick Access toolbar and choose Quick Print from the menu. **See also** "Working with the Quick Access Toolbar," in Part 1.

Selecting a Printer

If you have access to more than one printer, you may need to select the correct printer before printing. To do so, follow these steps:

1. Click the Office button and then click the left portion of the Print option (the portion with the title). Excel displays the Print dialog box.

2. In the Name drop-down list box, select the printer.

3. Click OK to close the dialog box.

The Print dialog box also lists information about the selected printer, such as its status and where it is connected.

Setting Sheet Printing Options

In most cases, you want to print the worksheet as displayed on-screen. Sometimes, however, you may want to control how or what elements get printed. Excel provides several options that allow you to control the appearance of your worksheet printouts.

Printing gridlines or row and column headings

Follow these steps to control the printing of gridlines or row and column headings:

1. Click the Page Layout tab on the Ribbon.

2. Do one or both of the following:

   • To print or suppress printing of gridlines, select or deselect the Print check box under the Gridlines heading in the Sheet Options group.

   • To print or suppress printing of row and column headings, select or deselect the Print check box under the Headings heading in the Sheet Options group.

Printing row or column data labels on each page

Worksheet data is often set up with labels (titles) in the first row and sometimes descriptive names in the first column. If such a worksheet requires more than one page to print, you may find reading subsequent pages difficult because the text in the first row or first column or both doesn't print on subsequent pages. Excel offers an option that allows you to print row and column labels (titles) on every page.

Follow these steps to select the row or column labels that will appear on each page:

1. Click the Page Layout tab on the Ribbon and then click the Print Titles button. Excel displays the Page Setup dialog box with the Sheet tab selected.

2. Click inside the appropriate box in the Print Titles area, and point to the row(s) or column(s) in the worksheet that you want to repeat on each page. You can also enter these references manually. For example, to specify rows 1 and 2 as repeating rows, enter **1:2**.

3. Click OK to close the Page Setup dialog box.

Remember: Don't confuse print titles with headers; these are two different concepts. Headers appear at the top of each page and contain information such as the worksheet name, date, or page number. Print titles describe the data that you're printing, such as field names in a table.

You can specify different print titles for each worksheet in the workbook. Excel remembers print titles by creating sheet-level names (Print_Titles).

Selecting miscellaneous sheet printing options

Excel provides some worksheet print options that you might use occasionally. Follow these steps to access these options:

1. Click the Page Layout tab on the Ribbon and click the dialog launcher button on the bottom right of the Sheet Options group container. Excel displays the Page Setup dialog box with the Sheet tab selected.

2. Select among these options:

   • **Black and White:** If you have a colorful worksheet but your printer is stuck in a monochrome world, you may discover that the worksheet colors don't translate well to black and white. In this case, you can use this option to instruct Excel to ignore the colors while printing.

   • **Draft Quality:** Printing in Draft mode doesn't print embedded charts or drawing objects, cell gridlines, or borders. This mode usually reduces the printing time and is handy for getting a quick printout.

- **Comments:** If one or more cells in your worksheet have a cell comment, you can print these comments along with the worksheet by choosing an option from the Comments drop-down list. By default, comments are not printed.

- **Errors:** Excel gives you the option to print error values as they appear on your worksheet or to replace each of the error values with a predefined character in the printed output. Error values include #NUM!, #DIV/0!, #REF!, #N/A, #VALUE!, #NAME?, and #NULL!. Choose an option from the Cell Errors As drop-down list. By default, errors are printed as displayed.

- **Page Order:** If you have a worksheet that spans across several columns and down several rows, your worksheet is likely to end up with multiple vertical page breaks, horizontal page breaks, or both. In this case, you have the choice of printing your worksheet pages from left to right or from top to bottom. In the Page Order area, click the Down, Then Over radio button or the Over, Then Down radio button. By default, Excel prints down, then over.

3. Click OK to close the Page Setup dialog box.

Setting the Print Area

If you choose to print the active worksheet or multiple sheets, Excel prints the entire sheet or sheets — or just the range named Print_Area. Each worksheet can have a range named Print_Area. After you set the print area, Excel automatically creates the Print_Area name. Print_Area is a standard named range, so you can edit the range's reference manually if you like.

See also "Editing Names," in Part 6.

To set the print area, follow these steps:

1. Select the range that you want to print. Press and hold Ctrl to select non-adjacent ranges.

2. Click the Page Layout tab on the Ribbon, click the Print Area button, and choose Set Print Area from the menu.

Remember: After you specify a print area, by default Excel uses that print area in all subsequent printouts. If you want to clear the print area (so that Excel automatically prints the entire worksheet,) click the Print Area button and choose Clear Print Area from the menu.

If you don't want to clear the normal print areas you create but occasionally want to ignore the print areas (to print the entire worksheet) select the Ignore Print Areas check box in the Print dialog box. To display the Print dialog box, click the Office button and then click the left portion of the Print option.

Specifying What You Want to Print

Excel gives you several options to determine the range of data in your worksheet or workbook that is printed. To tell Excel what data to print, follow these steps:

1. Click the Office button and select the left portion of the Print option (the portion with the title) from the menu. Excel displays the Print dialog box.

2. In the Print What area of the Print dialog box, specify what you want to print by selecting a radio button. You have the following four options:

   • **Selection:** Prints only the range that you select on the worksheet prior to displaying the Print dialog box in Step 1. Note that if you select non-contiguous ranges to print, Excel prints each range on a new sheet of paper.

   • **Active Sheet(s):** Prints the active sheet or all sheets that you select. You can select multiple sheets by pressing and holding Ctrl and clicking the sheet tabs. If you select multiple sheets, each sheet begins printing on a new page. This option is Excel's default print mode.

   • **Entire Workbook:** Prints the entire workbook, including worksheets and chart sheets.

   • **Table:** This option is available only if you have tables in your Worksheet. *See also* Part 11, "Working with Tables."

3. If you want to print only selected pages of your choice in Step 2, click the Page(s) option in the Print Range section of the dialog box, and specify the number of the first and last pages to print. You can use the spinner controls, or you can type the page numbers in the boxes. Note that you can select only a contiguous range of pages.

4. Click OK to start printing.

Part 10

Charting Your Data

A chart (also known as a *graph* outside Excel circles) is a way to present a table of numbers visually. The visual display allows you, for example, to quickly examine trends or compare the relative contributions of various items. Excel provides you with the tools to create a variety of charts.

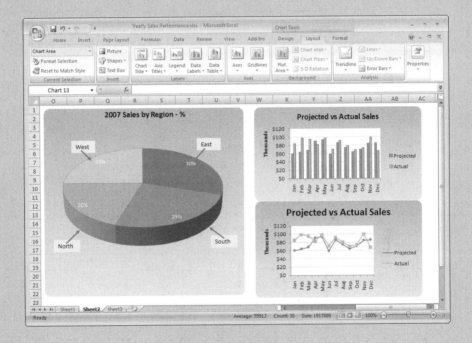

In this part . . .

- ✔ Adding a New Data Series to a Chart
- ✔ Changing the Chart Type for an Existing Chart or Data Series
- ✔ Chart Elements
- ✔ Creating a Chart
- ✔ Formatting a Chart Element
- ✔ Modifying a Chart Axis

Anatomy of a Chart

Before you create your first chart in Excel, it helps to know the elements that you can include in the chart. Figure 10-1 illustrates the most common elements that a chart can contain. When you create a chart, include only the elements you need to clearly portray your data. Too much information will make the chart hard to read and reduce its usefulness.

The following is a description of the elements shown in Figure 10-1:

✔ **Horizontal axis:** For most charts, this axis displays category labels. A category is any item without numerical significance. Month, Quarter, and Product are examples of categories. For a Month category, the labels might be Jan, Feb, Mar, and so on. The chart displays the labels at equally spaced intervals on the axis. For the bar, X Y scatter, and bubble chart types, the horizontal axis displays a value scale. A chart can have a *primary* horizontal axis and a *secondary* horizontal axis.

Primary vertical axis title

Chart area   Chart title   Tick mark

Primary vertical axis   Secondary vertical axis | Secondary vertical axis title

Plot area   Data label   Gridlines

Figure 10-1

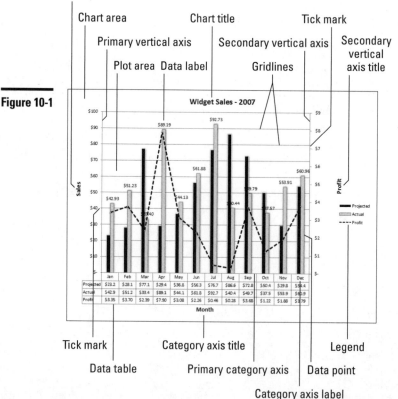

Tick mark | Category axis title   Legend

Data table   Primary category axis | Data point

Category axis label

- ✔ **Horizontal axis title:** Displays a name for the category plotted.

- ✔ **Vertical axis:** For most charts, this axis displays a value scale for the data series plotted. For the bar chart type, the vertical axis displays category labels. A chart can have a *primary* vertical axis and a *secondary* vertical axis.

- ✔ **Vertical axis title:** Displays a name for the value scale against which the series is plotted.

- ✔ **Data series:** A group of values associated with a category. For example, projected sales and actual sales might be two series associated with a Month category.

- ✔ **Data point:** A value associated with a category label. For example, projected and actual sales figures plotted for January represent data points.

- ✔ **Data labels:** Labels associated with the data points on the chart. For example the labels can be the values of data points.

- ✔ **Data table:** The data series represented in tabular form and placed directly below the horizontal axis.

- ✔ **Chart title:** A title that you provide for the chart.

- ✔ **Legend:** A group of keys and text identifying each data series in the chart.

- ✔ **Gridlines:** Lines placed on the chart to assist in reading the value of data points or to segregate category labels. Gridlines can be distracting and therefore should be used sparingly. If you must use gridlines, we suggest that you choose a pale and unobtrusive color for the line.

- ✔ **Tick marks:** These mark off intervals on an axis.

- ✔ **Plot area:** The area of the chart, defined by the axes boundaries, where the data series is plotted.

- ✔ **Chart area:** The entire area that includes all elements within the chart.

Activating a Chart

Before you can do anything with a chart, you must activate it, as follows:

- ✔ To activate a chart on a chart sheet, click the chart sheet's tab.

- ✔ To activate a chart that you embed in a worksheet, click the chart border area.

After you activate an embedded chart or a chart on a chart sheet, Excel displays the Chart Tools contextual tabs on the Ribbon. Double-clicking the chart automatically displays the Design tab tools on the Ribbon.

Adding a New Data Series to a Chart

Follow these steps to add a new data series to a chart:

1. Activate the chart, click the Design contextual tab and then click the Select Data button. Excel displays the Select Data Source dialog box (see Figure 10-2).

Figure 10-2

2. Click the Add button. Excel displays the Edit Series dialog box.

3. If the reference in the Series Name box is incorrect, clear the default entry and either type a name for the series or click the cell on the worksheet containing the series name. You can also leave the box blank.

4. If the reference in the Series Values box is incorrect, clear the default entry and select the series data range on the worksheet.

5. Click OK to return to the Select Data Source dialog box. The new series name (or a generic title if you didn't include a name in Step 3) appears in the legend entries window. In the window on the right side of the dialog box, Excel displays numbered category labels for the series. You can ignore these labels — Excel simply adds the new series to the chart using the existing category labels.

6. Click OK.

Another way to add a new data series to a chart is to select the range that you want to add (including any label for the series name), and click the Copy button on the Ribbon's Home tab. Then activate the chart, click the arrow on the Paste button, and choose Paste Special from the menu. Excel responds by opening the Paste Special dialog box. Complete the information in this dialog box to correspond to the data you selected.

Adding a Title to a Chart

The chart title normally appears at the top of the chart. When you create a chart, you can select a layout that includes a chart title box. To add a title to an existing chart, follow these steps:

1. Activate the chart and click the Layout tab to display the chart layout tools on the Ribbon.

2. Click the Chart Title button, and then choose an option from the menu. Excel adds a chart title box to the chart.

3. Click in the title box and type a title for the chart.

4. If you want to format the chart title, you can use the standard formatting options in the Font Group of the Ribbon's Home tab or you can use special WordArt and other formatting options in the Format tab.

Changing the Axes for a Data Series

Sometimes, you may want to plot two or more series that vary considerably in scale, such as Revenue and Profit. If you plot both series using the same axis, the profit figures will not appear clearly on the chart. In such cases, you can plot the revenue figures on the primary vertical axis (the default) and the profit figures on the secondary vertical axis (see Figure 10-1.)

Follow these steps to plot a data series on the secondary axis:

1. Select the series on the chart that will be plotted on the secondary axis. *See* "Selecting a Chart Element." later in this part.

2. Access the Format dialog box for the data series. *See* "Formatting a Chart Element," later in this part.

3. In the Plot Series On area of the Format Data Series dialog box, select the Secondary Axis option and then click Close. The secondary value axis appears on the chart. By default, Excel does not display the secondary category axis.

4. If you need to make adjustments to the primary or secondary axis, click the Layout tab, click the Axes button, click the axis you want to adjust, and choose an axis option from the flyout menu. *See also* "Modifying a Chart Axis," later in this part.

Remember: When you plot a series on the secondary axes, the series appears *over* the series plotted on the primary axes. Depending on the chart type you select, the series plotted on the secondary axis can obscure part or all of the series plotted on the primary axis if you are not careful.

Changing the Chart Type for an Existing Chart or Data Series

Excel supports a wide variety of chart types (line charts, column charts, and so on). After you create a chart, you might decide that a different chart type would better portray the data. You can even create a *combination* chart by selecting a different chart type for a data series. You can, for example, create a chart with one data series plotted as a line chart type and another data series plotted as a column chart type (see Figure 10-1).

To change the chart type for an existing chart or to change the chart type for a data series on a chart, follow these steps:

1. Activate the chart and click the Design tab to display the chart design tools on the Ribbon.

2. To change the chart type for the chart (this is, for all data series in the chart), click the Change Chart Type button. To change the chart type for a single data series, select the data series before clicking the Change Chart Type button. Excel displays the Change Chart Type dialog box.

3. In the list on the left, choose a chart type. Then in the gallery on the right, choose a chart subtype.

4. Click OK.

Creating a Chart

Creating professional looking charts is easier to do in Excel 2007 than in earlier versions. Excel 2007 provides several professionally designed layout and formatting gallery options that you can apply without having to start from scratch. Follow these steps to chart your data:

1. Select the data you want to chart, including any row and column labels (for category and series name identification).

2. Click the Insert tab on the Ribbon and then click a Chart Type button in the Charts group. Excel displays a chart subtype gallery.

3. Choose a subtype from the gallery. If you hover the mouse pointer over a chart type button or chart subtype gallery option, Excel displays a ScreenTip that provides assistance on how you can use the particular chart type or subtype.

   After you choose a subtype, Excel creates a chart and displays the chart tools contextual tabs on the Ribbon and a header on the Excel title bar above the tabs. Excel automatically displays the tools for the Design tab on the ribbon (see Figure 10-3).

Figure 10-3

4. If the layout of elements on the chart that Excel creates isn't what you want, choose a new layout from the Chart Layouts gallery. Use the upper arrows on the right side of the gallery to scroll the gallery display or the bottom arrow to display the entire gallery. Each layout includes a combination of elements for the chart. If you choose a layout that includes a chart title, click in the title box and type a title for the chart.

5. If required, select a new style for the chart from the Chart Styles gallery. Use the upper arrows on the right side of the gallery to scroll the gallery display or the bottom arrow to display the entire gallery. The styles in the gallery are based on the theme currently applied in the workbook, so if you change the theme, the styles change to match the new theme. ***See also*** "Formatting with Themes," in Part 1.

Figure 10-4 illustrates some important rules that Excel applies when creating a chart:

   ✔ If the data you're charting contains more rows than columns, Excel uses the row data to create the category axis. The row labels are used for category labels and the column labels are used for series names (in Figure 10-4, see the data range A1:D13 and the resultant chart on the right of the range.)

If the row labels are missing or not included in the range, Excel labels the category axis with numbers. If, in addition, the column labels are missing or not included in the range, Excel names the series as Series 1, Series 2, and so on. (In Figure 10-4, see the data range A15:C26 and the resultant chart on the right of the range.)

Figure 10-4

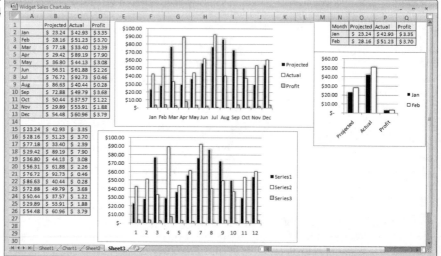

✔ If the data you're charting contains more columns than rows, or an equal number of columns and rows, Excel uses the column data to create the category axis. The column labels are used for category labels and the row labels are used for series names (in Figure 10-4, see the data range N1:Q3 and the resultant chart at the bottom of the range).

✔ If the data you're charting contains only one series, Excel includes a chart title with the same name as the series name, assuming that a row or column label is available for the series name (as per the first rule).

Remember: You can reverse Excel's category and series name choices after the chart is created by activating the chart and clicking the Switch Row/Column button on the Design tab.

Creating and Using a Chart Template

A *chart template* is a standard chart (or combination chart) customized in a specific manner. You can subsequently use the template to create new charts. To customize a chart that you can save as a template, following these steps:

1. Create a chart that's customized the way you want. For example, you can set colors or line styles, modify fonts and type sizes, add 3-D and shadow effects, and add a title.

2. Activate the chart and click the Design tab to display the chart design tools on the Ribbon.

3. Click the Save as Template button. Excel displays the Save Chart Template dialog box.

4. In the File Name box, enter a filename.

5. Click Save.

The template appears in the Templates category of the Change Chart Type dialog box (accessed by clicking the Change Chart Type button in the Design tab). After you select the Templates category, the new chart appears in the My Templates gallery on the right side of the dialog box. If you hover the mouse pointer over the chart, a ScreenTip displays the chart name you supplied in Step 4.

To use a template, *see* "Creating a Chart," earlier in this part, and choose the template from the Templates category.

Displaying a Data Table in a Chart

In Excel, you can display a table of the data that you use in the chart. The data table appears below the chart (see Figure 10-1). When you create a chart, you can select a layout that includes a data table.

To add a data table to an existing chart, follow these steps:

1. Activate the chart and click the Layout tab to display the chart layout tools on the Ribbon.

2. Click the Data Table button and choose an option from the menu. The data table appears below the chart.

3. To explore additional formatting options for the data table, choose More Data Table Options from the menu. Excel displays the Format Data Table dialog box.

4. Make your selections from the various formatting options and click OK.

Displaying Data Labels in a Chart

Sometimes you want your chart to display the data value for each point on the chart (see Figure 10-1). Or you want to display the category label for each data point. When you create a chart, you can select a layout that includes data labels.

To add data labels to a chart series, follow these steps:

1. Activate the chart and click the Layout tab to display the chart layout tools on the Ribbon.

2. Click one of the data points in the series. This action selects the entire data series.

After you select the entire series, be careful not to click a data point because this action selects only a single data point. If you do accidentally select a single data point, click anywhere outside the data series and repeat this step.

3. Click the Data Labels button and choose an option from the menu. The data labels appear on the chart.

4. To explore additional formatting options for the data labels:

   a. Choose More Data Label Options from the menu. Excel displays the Format Data Labels dialog box.

   b. Make your selections from the various formatting options.

   c. Click OK.

Remember: The data labels are linked to the worksheet, so if your data changes, the labels change too. To override the data label with some other text, select the label and enter the new text (or even a cell reference) in the formula bar.

If Excel doesn't position the data labels correctly, you can select an individual label and drag it to a better location. To select an individual label, click the label twice.

Formatting a Chart Element

You can modify the elements in a chart in several ways. For example, you can change colors, line widths, and fonts. You make modifications in the Format dialog box, which varies for each type of chart element.

To modify an element in a chart, follow these steps:

1. Select the chart element. *See* "Selecting a Chart Element," later in this part.

2. Access the Format dialog box for the chart element that you selected by using any of the following techniques:

   - Click the Format tab on the Ribbon and select a chart element from the Chart Elements drop-down list in the Current Selection group. Then click the Format Selection button below the Chart Elements list.

   - Right-click the element, and choose Format *Item Name* from the contextual menu that appears, where *Item Name* is the name of the chart element you select, such as Data Series, Gridlines, or Axis.

   - Press Ctrl+1 (that is, Ctrl and the number 1).

3. Choose the option on the left side of the dialog box that corresponds to what you want to do.

4. Make the changes by selecting the appropriate options on the right side of the dialog box. For help on an option, click the Help button (the question mark) in the dialog box.

5. Click OK.

Remember: You can change the color of some element parts — for example, the fill color or line color. You can select a theme color or a non-theme color. If you choose a theme color, the color changes if you change the workbook theme. If you choose a non-theme color, the color does not change if you change the workbook theme. *See also* "Formatting with Themes," in Part 1.

Handling Missing Data or Charting Hidden Data

Sometimes, data that you're charting may be missing one or more data points. Also, by default, Excel does not include data in hidden rows and columns within the data range you're charting. Excel offers several options for handling the missing data and allows you to chart hidden data in a range. Just follow these steps:

1. Activate the chart and click the Design tab to display the chart design tools on the Ribbon.

2. Click the Select Data button. Excel displays the Select Data Source dialog box.

3. Click the Hidden and Empty Cells button. Excel displays the Hidden and Empty Cell Settings dialog box.

4. Select the option that corresponds to how you want to handle the missing data:

   - **Gaps:** Excel ignores missing data, and the data series leaves a gap for each missing data point. This is the default setting.

   - **Zero:** Excel treats missing data as zero.

   - **Connect Data Points with Line:** Excel calculates missing data by using data on either side of the missing point(s). This option is available only for line charts and some X Y scatter chart subtypes.

5. If you want to chart hidden data within the chart's source data range, select the Show Data in Hidden Rows and Columns check box.

6. Click OK to exit the Hidden and Empty Cell Settings dialog box, and click OK again to exit the Select Data Source dialog box.

Remember: The options that you set apply to the entire active chart; you can't set a different option for different series in the same chart.

Inserting and Modifying Chart Legends

A *legend* explains the data series in a chart. A legend consists of text and keys. A *key* is a small graphic that corresponds to the chart's series.

Adding a legend to a chart

When you create a chart, you can select a layout that includes a legend (see Figure 10-1). If you don't include a legend as you create the chart, you can add one later. To add a legend to an existing chart, follow these steps:

1. Activate the chart and click the Layout tab to display the chart layout tools on the Ribbon.

2. Click the Legend button and choose an option from the menu. Excel displays the legend on the chart.

Changing the names (titles) on a chart legend

If you don't include row or column titles with the source data when you create a chart, Excel displays the default names (titles) *Series 1, Series 2,* and so on in the legend. To change the default names, follow these steps:

1. Activate the chart and click the Design tab to display the chart design tools on the Ribbon.

2. Click the Select Data button. You can also right-click the border area of the chart and choose Select Data from the contextual menu. Excel displays the Select Data Source dialog box.

3. Choose one of the *Series 1, Series 2* and so on names in the Legend Entries (Series) window, and then click the Edit button above the series name. Excel displays the Edit Series dialog box.

4. Clear the entry in the Series Name box and either type a new name or point to a worksheet cell containing the name you want to use. Click OK to add the name and return to the Select Data Source dialog box.

5. Repeat Step 4 for each series that you want to rename.

6. Click OK to exit the Select Data Source dialog box.

Modifying a Chart Axis

After you create a chart, you may want the modify the value axis to change the scale, add an axis title, modify the tick mark display, add display units, and so on. Or you may want to modify the category axis to, for example, add a title, modify the tick marks, or change where the axis crosses the value axis.

Follow these steps to modify a chart axis:

1. Activate the chart and click the Layout tab to display the chart layout tools on the Ribbon.

2. Click the Axes button and choose a Horizontal Axis or Vertical Axis option, depending on which axis you want to modify. After you chose an axis option, a flyout menu appears.

3. If one of the standard options on the flyout menu is what you want, choose the option, and you've finished the procedure. Otherwise, continue at Step 4.

4. If none of the standard flyout menu options are what you want, choose More *<Axis>* Options at the bottom of the flyout menu, where *<Axis>* is the horizontal or vertical axis. Excel displays the Format Axis dialog box.

5. On the right side of the dialog box, select the axis options you want to change. For help, click the help button (the question mark at the top-right of the dialog box).

You may have to experiment with the options to get what you want. You can always undo your selections (by clicking the undo button on the Quick Access toolbar) and start over if your chart doesn't show the expected results.

6. If you want to modify the axis formatting (number, fill, line, and so on), select one or more of the options in the list on the left side of the dialog box and select the appropriate options on the right.

7. Click OK when you are finished making your selections.

To add a title to an axis, activate the chart, select the Layout tab and click the Axis titles button. Choose an axis from the menu and choose a title option from the flyout menu. After Excel displays the axis title box on the chart, click in the box and enter a title.

Resizing, Moving, Copying, and Deleting an Embedded Chart

To resize an embedded chart, follow these steps:

1. Activate the chart.

2. Drag one of the eight resize handles (a series of dots) on the chart border to change the size of the element. When you hover the mouse pointer over a resize handle or when you drag the resize handle, the pointer changes into a black line with arrows on both ends.

You can move the embedded chart to a different location on the worksheet or you can make a copy of the chart on the worksheet:

✔ To move a chart, first activate it. Then click the border of the chart between the resize handles, and drag the chart to the desired location in the worksheet. When you hover the mouse pointer over a border or when you drag the border, the pointer changes into a white arrow with a black cross on the arrow's tip.

✔ To copy a chart, activate it. Then press and hold down the Ctrl key while dragging the chart. You can also use the Copy and Paste buttons on the Ribbon's Home tab or press Ctrl+C to copy and Ctrl+V to paste.

✔ To move the embedded chart to a separate chart sheet, select the chart, click the Design tab, and then click the Move Chart button. Specify the new location in the Move Chart dialog box, and click OK. A chart sheet typically contains a single chart that is linked to the data in the worksheet.

To delete a chart, activate the chart and press the Delete key.

Resizing, Moving, and Deleting a Chart Element

You can resize the following chart elements: any of the titles, the data labels, the legend, and the plot area. To resize a chart element, follow these steps:

1. Select the chart element that you want to resize.

2. Drag a resize handle (a square box or a circle) on the element border to change the size of the element. When you hover the mouse pointer over a resize handle, the pointer changes to a double-headed arrow. Clicking the mouse to drag the handle changes the pointer to a cross.

You can move the titles, the data labels, and the legend within the chart area. To move a chart element, follow these steps:

1. Select the chart element that you want to move.

2. Click the border of the element between the resize handles, and drag the element to the desired location in the chart. When you hover the mouse pointer over a border or when you drag the border, the pointer changes to a cross with an arrow on each end.

You can delete any element in a chart, including a data series. To delete a chart element, follow these steps:

1. Select the element that you want to delete.

2. Press the Delete key.

See also "Selecting a Chart Element," immediately following this section.

Selecting a Chart Element

Modifying an element in a chart is similar to everything else that you do in Excel: First you make a selection — in this case, select a chart element — and then you issue a command to do something with the selection.

You can select a chart element in any of the following three ways:

✔ Click the chart element. If the element is a series, clicking the series once selects all the points in the series. Clicking the series twice selects individual points in the series.

✔ Press the up-arrow or down-arrow key to cycle through all the elements in the chart. If a data series is selected, you can press the right-arrow or left-arrow key to select individual points in the series.

✔ Click the Format tab on the Ribbon and select a chart element from the Chart Elements drop-down list (located above the Format Selection button) in the Current Selection group.

 TIP If you move the mouse pointer over a chart element, a ScreenTip displays the name of the element. If the element is a data point, the ScreenTip displays the value. The ScreenTip is useful in ensuring that you're selecting the intended element.

Updating the Source Data Range for a Chart or a Data Series

Often, you create a chart that uses a particular range of data, and then you extend the data range by adding new data in the worksheet. If you add new data to a range, the data series in the chart doesn't update to include the new data. Or you may delete some of the data in a range that you used to create the chart. If you delete data from a range, by default the chart displays the deleted data as zero values.

To update the entire chart to reflect the new data range, follow these steps:

1. Activate the chart, and then click the Design tab to display the chart design tools on the Ribbon.

2. Click the Select Data button. Excel displays the Select Data Source dialog box.

3. In the Chart Data Range box, manually edit the source data reference or clear the box and use the mouse pointer to select the new range on the worksheet.

4. Click OK, and Excel updates the chart with the new data range.

If you need to update the range for a single data series on the chart, follow these steps:

1. Activate the chart, and then click the Design tab to display the chart design tools on the Ribbon.

2. Click the Select Data button. Excel displays the Select Data Source dialog box.

3. Select the series name of the series you want to modify in the Legend Entries (Series) window, and click the Edit button above the window. Excel displays the Edit Series dialog box.

4. In the Series Values box, manually edit the source data reference, or clear the box and use the mouse pointer to select the new range on the worksheet. Click OK to return to the Select Data Source dialog box.

5. If necessary, modify the range for category labels. Click the Edit button under Horizontal (Categories) Axis Labels to display the Axis Labels dialog box. In the Axis Label Range box, manually edit the category labels reference, or clear the box and select the new range on the worksheet.

6. Click OK, and Excel updates the chart with the new data range.

After you activate a chart, Excel outlines in the worksheet the ranges that the chart uses. To extend or reduce the range of the entire chart, simply drag an outline handle (a small square box on the corner of the outline). To extend or reduce the range of a data series, select the data series in the chart and drag an outline handle.

A better way to handle data ranges that change is to convert the range to a *table*. After you add or remove data from a table, the chart created from the range (either before or after you convert the range to a table) updates automatically. ***See also*** Part 11, "Working with Tables."

Using and Changing the Default Chart Type

The default chart is the type that Excel creates if you don't specify the type. Excel's default chart type is a 2-D clustered column chart that uses Layout 11 from the Chart Layouts gallery and Style 13 from the Chart Styles gallery. To use the default chart type after selecting your source data, do one of the following:

✔ To create the default chart on the worksheet (an embedded chart), press Alt+F1.

✔ To create the default chart on a chart sheet, press F11.

If you often use a different type of chart, you may want to change the default type as follows:

1. Activate the chart and click the Design tab to display the chart design tools on the Ribbon.

2. Click the Change Chart Type button. Excel displays the Change Chart Type dialog box.

3. Choose a chart type in the list on the left and choose a chart subtype in the gallery on the right.

4. Click the Set as Default Chart button and then click OK. The new default chart will be used for all default charts in all workbooks.

You can also use a chart template as a default chart type. *See* "Creating and Using a Chart Template," earlier in this part.

Part 11

Working with Tables

A *table* is structure that allows you to conveniently analyze data and generate professional looking reports. Data for the table can be entered manually, copied from another worksheet (in the same or different workbook in which you create the table), or imported from external sources such as a text file, the Web, an XML file, or a database file.

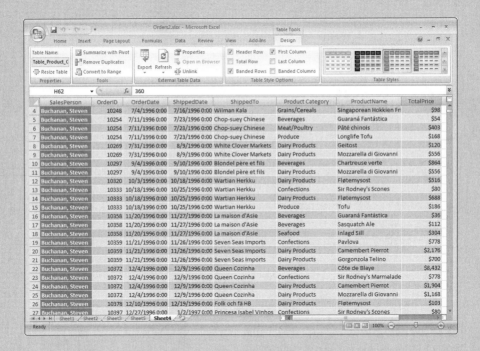

In this part . . .

- ✔ **Creating a Table**
- ✔ **Filtering Data in a Table**
- ✔ **Formatting a Table**
- ✔ **Removing Duplicate Values from a Table**
- ✔ **Sorting Data in a Table**

Anatomy of a Table

The *table* feature included in Excel 2007 (see Figure 11-1) is an extension of the list feature found in earlier versions of Excel. Excel 2007 provides many convenient tools that allow you to analyze data in a table and generate professional looking reports. For example, you can easily sort and filter data, format the table using a gallery of styles, add rows, add a totals row, add formula columns, and create charts and PivotTables that automatically update after rows are added or removed. You create the data for the table manually, copy the data from a worksheet, link the data from a worksheet or a different workbook, or import the data from an external source. If the data in your worksheet is arranged like that shown in Figure 11-1 — that is, a list of information — consider converting the list to a table to take advantage of a table's many convenient features. *See also* "Creating a Table," later in this part.

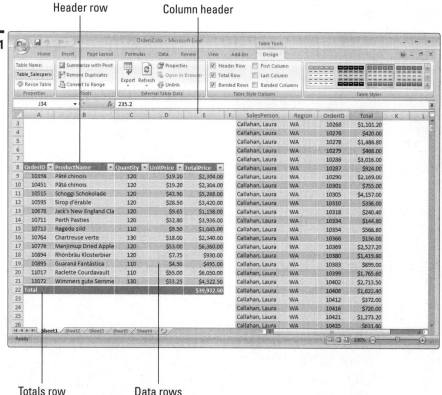

Figure 11-1

Header row
Column header
Totals row
Data rows

The following is a description of the parts of a table:

- ✔ **Table area:** The header row, data rows, and optional totals row.

- ✔ **Header row:** Names shared by all data rows — for example, Customer Name, Order ID, and Unit Price.

- ✔ **Data row:** Specific information derived from the columns in the header row, such as transaction information (for example, details of sales), customer data, or product data.

- ✔ **Totals row:** Allows you to perform a calculation (such as Sum, Average, or Count) on any column of data.

Tables often contain more rows that can be displayed simultaneously on the screen. If the cell pointer is within the table and you scroll the worksheet so that the header row is no longer displayed in the worksheet window, the header titles appear in the column header area (see Figure 11-1). *See also* "Familiarizing Yourself with the Excel 2007 Window," in Part 1.

Converting a Table to a Range

If you no longer need to work with a table, you can convert the table to a normal range. Right-click in the table and choose Table⇨Convert to Range from the contextual menu or click anywhere in the table and then click Convert to Range in the Table Tools Design tab.

Creating a Table

You can create a table from a data range that is set up with a header row. If your range does not include a header row, you should add one. *See also* Part 4, "Entering and Editing Worksheet Data." Follow these steps to create a table from a range:

1. Select any cell in the range.

2. Click the Insert tab on the Ribbon and then click the Table button (or press Ctrl+L). Excel displays the Create Table dialog box and selects the entire contiguous range that includes the active cell pointer.

3. Click OK. Excel creates the table, applies a default style, and adds a sort and filter arrow to the cells in the header row. Excel also displays the Table Tools Design tab on the Ribbon.

Filtering Data in a Table

Filtering data is one of the most common activities performed with a table. Often, you want to view or analyze a subset of the data in a large dataset. When Excel creates a table, it includes a sort and filter drop-down arrow to the right of each column header. After you filter your table, the status bar displays the number of rows visible.

Remember: You can use Excel's filtering features in a standard (non-table) range. Select the range, click the Sort & Filter button on the Ribbon's home tab, and choose Filter from the menu to add the sort and filter drop-down arrows to the header row. A worksheet can have only one sort and filter range but can have many tables, each with its own sort and filter settings.

Remember: If your table data was imported from an external range, your table filters and sort orders are normally reapplied after you refresh the range (import the latest data). If you add data rows manually, however, you must click the Sort & Filter button in the Ribbon's Home tab and then choose Reapply from the menu before Excel will update the table.

Filtering based on individual column entries

Follow these steps to filter your table data based on the individual entries in a column:

1. Click the arrow on the header of the column you want to filter. Excel displays the Sort and Filter menu (see Figure 11-2).

Figure 11-2

2. The lower portion of the menu displays the *unique* column entries in a window. By default, Excel selects all entries. If you want to display rows for one or only a few entries, clear the Select All check box and individually select the items you want displayed. Alternatively, if you want to *hide* rows for only a few entries, clear the check boxes next to these entries but do not clear the Select All check box.

The ability to select multiple column entries is new in Excel 2007. Also, the list can display up to 10,000 unique entries (compared with 1000 entries in earlier versions of Excel).

3. Click OK. In the table, Excel displays rows for all the entries you selected in Step 2 and hides all rows for the cleared entries. If your table uses an alternative row-banding style, the banding is preserved after you filter table rows. Excel also adds a filter icon (a small funnel) on the column drop-down to indicate that a filter is applied to the column.

4. To filter additional columns, repeat Steps 2 and 3.

If your column has a series of date entries (month, day, year), Excel allows you to filter at the year, month, or day levels. In the column items list window, only the year level is listed initially. If you click the plus sign (+) next to a year, the months for that year are listed. Clicking the plus sign next to the month displays individual day entries for that month.

Filtering based on column data type

Suppose you have a table column that contain dates. But instead of filtering the column based on individual dates, you want to display dates for the current month, last month, last quarter, or year to date. Or suppose you have a numeric column and want to display records exceeding a certain value or lying between two values. Or perhaps you have a text column and you want to display records that begin with certain text or contain certain text. Excel 2007 provides many filtering options that you can apply based on the type of data you have in a column.

To filter a table data based on date, number, or text criteria, follow these steps:

1. Click the arrow on the header of the column you want to filter. Excel displays the filter and sort menu.

2. Immediately above the window that displays individual column entries, choose the *datatype* Filters option (where *datatype* is Text, Number, or Date, depending on the data type of the column you're filtering).

3. Choose a specific filter option from the flyout menu or choose Custom Filter at the bottom of the menu to display a dialog box that offers additional options.

4. If your choice in Step 3 displays a dialog box, complete the dialog box options and click OK.

Filtering based on cell color

Excel 2007 allows you to filter by cell color. Colors are cell background or font colors applied manually or by conditional formatting. Colors can also include color scales and icon sets. *See also* "Formatting based on cell or column content," later in this part.

Remember: You can filter by only one color at a time.

To filter your table data based on color formatting, follow these steps:

1. Click the arrow on the header of the column with the color formatting you want to filter. Excel displays the Sort and Filter menu.

2. Choose Filter by Color, and then choose a color option from the flyout menu. You can also choose the No Fill option to filter out all cells with font or background formatting.

Remember: Colors for filtering do *not* include colors defined in the table style, so your table formatting is preserved after color filtering.

Formatting a Table

When you create a table, Excel applies a default style to the table. However, you can apply a different predefined style to the table or create a style from scratch. You can also apply formatting based on the contents or a cell or table column.

Applying a new style to a table

Excel identifies the following specific areas in a table that you can format automatically and independently: the header row, data rows, totals row, first column, and last column. Follow these steps to apply a new style to a table:

1. Click any cell in the table and then click the Design tab.

2. Select a new style from the Table Styles gallery. You can scroll the gallery options by clicking the upper (scroll) arrows on the right side of the gallery, or you can display a drop-down grid by clicking the arrow below the scroll arrows. You can preview a style by hovering the mouse pointer over a style. Click a style option to apply a style.

3. In addition, or as an alternative, to Step 2, you can select style and display options from the Table Style Options group. Click to select or deselect the appropriate check boxes.

Remember: The styles you apply from the Table Styles gallery are based on the theme applied to the workbook. Therefore, if you change the workbook theme, both the table style and gallery styles change to match the new theme. *See also* "Formatting with Themes," in Part 1.

Formatting based on cell or column content

Formatting a table based on the contents of a cell or column contents (conditional formatting) is similar to formatting a non-table cell or range based on the contents of the cell or range. *See* "Formatting Based on the Contents of a Cell or Range," and "Formatting a Range Using Visualizations," both in Part 8. However, note the following when you apply conditional formatting to a table:

- For all formatting options except those involving visualizations, there is an option to format the corresponding table row when the format condition(s) in a cell(s) is true.

- If you apply conditional formatting to an entire column, the formatting for the column is automatically extended if you add new rows to the table.

- Formatting is applied to a table in the following order: direct formatting (for example, formatting you apply from the Font group in the Ribbon's Home tab) appears over table style formatting and conditional formatting appears over direct formatting.

Inserting a Totals Row in a Table

When you create a table, by default Excel does not include the totals row. However, if you need to total data in your table columns, you can add a totals row easily. Make sure that the cell pointer is in the table range, click the Design tab, and select the Totals Row check box in the Table Style Options group.

After you click the mouse pointer in a cell of the totals row, Excel adds a drop-down arrow to the cell. Clicking the arrow displays a convenient list of common functions you can apply (Sum, Average, Count, Standard Deviation, and so on). You can also enter any formula you want.

Inserting and Deleting Table Rows and Columns

You may need to insert new rows into a table to add data. Also, you may want to add a column to perform a calculation based on other columns in the table. Excel provides convenient methods for inserting rows and columns. You can also delete table rows and columns you no longer need.

Adding and deleting table rows

Choose one of the following methods to rows to a table:

- ✔ To add a row above an existing table row (including the totals row), right-click a cell in the existing table row and choose Insert⇨ Table Rows Above. If you right-click a cell in the last data row, you can add a row above or below the last row.

- ✔ If you use the Tab key to move to the next column when entering data in a row, Excel adds a new row automatically after you press the Tab key in the rightmost column of the last data row.

- ✔ If a blank row is immediately below the last data row, you can enter data in any cell in the blank row and Excel will add the row to the table. Table formatting (normal and conditional) and any column formulas are extended to include the new row.

To delete a table row, right-click any cell in the row and choose Delete⇨Table Rows from the contextual menu. To delete multiple rows, select the rows, right-click within the selection and choose Delete⇨Table Rows.

Adding and deleting table columns

Choose one of the following methods to add columns to a table:

- ✔ To add a column to the left of an existing table column, right-click a cell in the existing table column, and then choose Insert⇨Table Columns to the Left from the contextual menu. If you right-click a cell in the rightmost table column, you can add a column to the left or right of the rightmost column. Excel provides a generic title for the column header that you can change to a more meaningful name.

- ✔ If a blank column is immediately to the right of the rightmost column, you can enter data in any cell in the blank column and Excel will add the column to the table. The table formatting is extended to the new column.

To delete a table column, right-click any cell in the column and choose Delete⇨ Table Columns from the contextual menu. To delete multiple columns, select the columns, right-click within the selection, and choose Delete⇨Table Columns.

Remember: You cannot add individual cells to or remove individual cells from a table. You can add or remove only entire rows or entire columns.

Referencing Table Data in a Formula

When you create a table, Excel provides a generic name for the table (*Table1*, *Table2* and so on). If you intend to reference table data in a formula, you should change the name to something more descriptive, such as *SalesData*. To change Excel's default table name, select any cell within the table, click the Design tab on the Ribbon, and enter a new name in the Table Name text box. Excel also allows you to use column name references in formulas. The following rules apply to table and column names:

- ✔ The table name must be different from any other names you create in the workbook and must follow Excel's name creation rules. ***See also*** Part 6, "Creating and Using Names."

- ✔ Column names must be unique within the table, although different tables can have the same column names.

- ✔ If a table name or column name changes, formulas that reference the name automatically update to include the new name.

- ✔ Excel updates table and column name references automatically as rows and columns are added or removed from the table.

Remember: You can save time entering table name references in a formula by using the Formula AutoComplete feature, which lists the names. ***See also*** "Entering formulas manually," in Part 4.

Referencing table data outside the table

When you reference table data in a formula that's outside the table range, the reference must include the table name. Use the following methods to reference table data in a formula:

- ✔ To reference all the data in the table, use the table name. If you want to sum all the data in a table named *SalesData*, for example, enter

```
=SUM(SalesData)
```

- ✔ To reference the data in a table column, use the table name and a column qualifier in the form *TableName[ColumnName]*. For example, if you want to sum a column named *Quarter1* in a table named *SalesData*, enter

```
=SUM(SalesData[Quarter1])
```

- Other table references are useful for some types of lookup formulas. To reference an entire table, use the form `TableName[#All]`. To reference table headers only, use the form `TableName[#Headers]`. To reference an entire column (header and data) use the form `TableName[[#All], [ColumnName]`. To reference just the header text of a column, use `TableName [[#Headers], [ColumnName]]`.

Referencing table data using a calculated column

A *calculated column* (sometimes called a *calculated field*), is simply a column you add to the table that references table data in a formula. The formula references are similar to those described in "Referencing table data outside the table," except that the table name is not required because the calculated column is part of the table. Follow these steps to add a calculated column and add a formula:

1. Add a new column to the table. ***See*** "Inserting and Deleting Table Rows and Columns," earlier in this part.

2. Enter a formula that references the table in any cell of the new column. You can enter the formula manually or by pointing with the mouse. For example, if you have a table named *SalesData* and you want to calculate the difference between the sales figures in columns named *Quarter1* and *Quarter2*, enter

   ```
   =[Quarter1]-[Quarter2]
   ```

   See Figure 11-3. You can use the Formula AutoComplete drop-down list to help speed up your entry. To enter the formula by pointing with the mouse, type the equal sign (=), point to the Quarter1 column in the *same* row as the formula you're entering, type the minus sign (–) and point to the Quarter2 column. As you type and point with the mouse, Excel completes the formula.

3. After you complete the formula, press Enter. Excel fills the entire column with the formula.

Figure 11-3

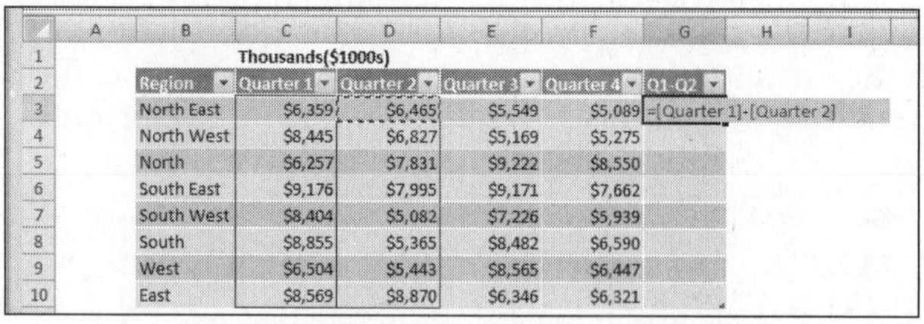

	A	B	C	D	E	F	G	H	I
1			Thousands($1000s)						
2		Region	Quarter 1	Quarter 2	Quarter 3	Quarter 4	Q1-Q2		
3		North East	$6,359	$6,465	$5,549	$5,089	=[Quarter 1]-[Quarter 2]		
4		North West	$8,445	$6,827	$5,169	$5,275			
5		North	$6,257	$7,831	$9,222	$8,550			
6		South East	$9,176	$7,995	$9,171	$7,662			
7		South West	$8,404	$5,082	$7,226	$5,939			
8		South	$8,855	$5,365	$8,482	$6,590			
9		West	$6,504	$5,443	$8,565	$6,447			
10		East	$8,569	$8,870	$6,346	$6,321			

Remember: If you change the formula in any cell of a calculated column, Excel updates the formulas in all other cells in the column automatically. If you do not want Excel to update all other cells in the column, click the Smart Tag (the light-ning bolt icon with the drop-down arrow) that appears next to the column after you update the formula and choose Undo Calculated Column from the menu.

Removing Duplicate Values from a Table

If you have a table with duplicated information, you might want to remove the rows containing the duplicates before analyzing the data. Excel provides many convenient options for removing duplicated data. For example, you can choose to remove duplicates if the entire row is duplicated (the default option) or you can choose to remove rows if the data in one or more columns is duplicated. Follow these steps to remove duplicated data from your table:

1. Click any cell in the table, and then click the Design tab on the Ribbon.

2. Click the Remove Duplicates button. Excel selects the entire data area of the table and displays the Remove Duplicates dialog box (see Figure 11-4).

Figure 11-4

3. If you want to remove rows in which all column data is duplicated, click OK. If you want to remove rows in which only data in one or more columns is duplicated (for example, a last name), select the column or columns and click OK.

The duplicated data is removed from the table permanently. If the result of the removal operation is not what you want, you can undo the operation (click the undo button on the Quick Access toolbar or press Ctrl+Z) and start over.

TIP If you want to retain your original data, you can select and copy the table to another worksheet. If you have a particularly large data range, make a copy of the worksheet.

Remember: You can remove duplicates in an ordinary (non-table) range. Select the range and click the Remove Duplicates button in the Ribbon's Data tab.

Selecting Table Areas

Excel 2007 provides convenient methods for you to select table rows, table columns, or the entire table. These methods are particularly useful if, for example, you want to copy table data or move the table to another location or format entire columns conditionally:

- To select a table row, move the mouse pointer to the leftmost column in the row until the pointer changes into a right-pointing arrow. Then click the mouse to select the row. You can select a table row also by selecting any cell in the row and pressing Shift+spacebar.

- To select the data cells in a table column, move the mouse pointer to the header row until the pointer changes into a down-pointing arrow. Then click the mouse to select the data cells. If you want to select the entire table column, including the header and totals cells, click the mouse again. You can select the data cells of a table column also by selecting any cell in the column and pressing Ctrl+spacebar. Pressing Ctrl+spacebar again selects the entire table column.

- To select all data rows in a table, move the mouse pointer to the upper-left cell in the header row until the mouse changes into a diagonal arrow, and then click to select the data rows. Click the mouse again to select the entire table. You can select all data rows in the table also by pressing Ctrl+Shift+spacebar. Press Ctrl+Shift+spacebar again to select the entire table. Another way to select the entire table is to select any cell in the table and move the mouse pointer to any edge of the table until the pointer changes to an arrow with a cross at the tip. Then click to select the table.

Sorting Data in a Table

Sorting a table involves rearranging the rows so they're in ascending or descending order, based on the values in one or more columns. You may, for example, want to sort a table of salespeople alphabetically by last name or by sales region. You can sort numerically, alphabetically, or by date, depending on the data.

If you sort a filtered table, Excel sorts only the visible rows. After you remove the filtering from the table, the table is no longer sorted. Therefore, you should remove any column filters before sorting the table.

Remember: You need to re-sort your table after adding (and perhaps editing) table rows. To re-sort the table, click any cell in the table, click the Sort & Filter button in the Design tab and choose Reapply from the menu. **See also** "Filtering Data in a Table," earlier in this part.

Sorting a single column based on column values

Follow these steps to sort a single column in your table based on the data in the table:

1. Click the arrow on the header of the column you want to sort. Excel displays the filter and sort menu.

2. Choose one of the sort direction options at the top of the menu. The options depend on the data type in the column you're sorting (numeric, text, or date). After you choose an option, Excel rearranges the rows in the table.

After you apply a sort to a column, Excel adds a small arrow to the column header arrow, indicating the direction of the sort. The arrow also serves as a reminder that you've applied a sort to the column.

The ability to sort by date order (that is, oldest to newest or newest to oldest) is new in Excel 2007.

Sorting multiple columns based on column values

Follow these steps to sort multiple columns in your table based on the data in the table:

1. Click the arrow on the header of any column in the table. Excel displays the filter and sort menu.

2. Choose Sort by Color and then choose Custom Sort from the flyout menu. Excel displays the Sort dialog box.

3. From the following drop-down lists, choose the options for the first column you want to sort:

   • Sort by: Choose the first column you want to sort by.

   • Sort on: Choose Values.

   • Order: Choose a sort order.

4. For each additional column you want to sort, click the Add Level button. Each time you do so, new drop-down lists appear. Repeat Step 3 for each sort level you add (see Figure 11-5).

Figure 11-5

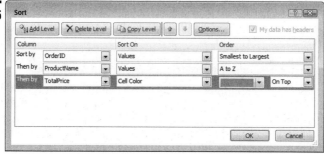

5. If you want your sorts to be case sensitive (applicable to text columns only), click the Options button and select the Case Sensitive check box. When you make your sorts case sensitive, uppercase letters appear before lowercase letters in an ascending sort. Normally, sorting ignores the case of letters.

6. If you want to change the sort order of a column after you add several sort levels, click the left side of the sort level and click the up or down arrow button. If you want to delete a sort level, click the left side of the sort level and click the Delete Level button. After you click a sort level, Excel highlights the level so you know which level you're deleting or reordering.

7. Click OK, and Excel rearranges the table's rows.

In Excel 2007, you can sort on up to 64 columns (up from 3 columns in earlier versions).

Sorting based on a custom sort order

In some cases, you may want to sort a text column in an order other than alphabetical ascending or descending. If your data consists of month names, for example, you probably want them to appear in month order rather than alphabetically. Excel has four custom lists, and you can also define your own. To sort one or more columns by a custom list, follow these steps:

1. Complete Steps 1–3 in "Sorting multiple columns based on column values," except in Step 3, choose Custom List from the Order drop-down list. Excel displays the Custom Lists dialog box.

2. In the Custom Lists box, choose a sort order list.

3. Click OK to add the custom list to the Order drop-down in the Sort dialog box.

4. Click OK. Excel rearranges the table's rows based on the custom order.

You can also create a custom list in the Custom Lists dialog box. To create a custom list, follow these steps:

1. In the Custom Lists box, select the New List entry.

2. In the List Entries text box, type your entries in the order you want your list sorted. Press Enter after you type each entry of the list, or separate each entry with a comma.

3. Click Add to include your new list in the Custom Lists box.

4. Click your new list and then click OK to add your list to the Order drop-down list in the Sort dialog box.

5. Click OK. Excel rearranges the table's rows based on your custom order.

Sorting based on color or conditional formatting icons

In Excel 2007, you can sort by background or font colors applied to cells manually or by conditional formatting. You can also sort by conditional formatting icon sets or color scales. Sorting by color is useful if you want to group data that meets a conditional formatting criterion.

Follow these steps to sort columns based on color (or icon):

1. Click the arrow on the header of the column that you want to sort by color (or icon). Excel displays the filter and sort menu.

2. If you want to sort by a single color, choose Sort by Color and choose a color (or icon, if applicable) from the flyout menu. After you choose a color option, Excel moves the rows with that color to the top of the table.

A quick way to sort by a single color is to right-click a cell in the column with the color, choose Sort from the contextual menu, and then choose an appropriate color sort option (cell color, cell font, or cell icon).

You can sort by more than one color if, for example, you have multiple colors in a column based on conditional formatting conditions or you want to arrange color scale colors or icon set icons in a particular order in a column. *See also* "Formatting a Range Using Visualizations," in Part 8, for a discussion of color scales and icon sets. Follow these steps to sort by more than one color in a column:

1. Complete the preceding steps to sort by the first color.

2. Click the arrow on the column header, choose Sort by Color and choose Custom Sort from the flyout menu. Excel displays the Sort dialog box with the first sort level listed (refer to Figure 11-5).

3. Click the left side of the existing sort level and click the Copy Level button. Excel adds a new sort level with identical sort conditions.

4. Click the Order drop-down list and choose a color (or icon if applicable) for the new sort level.

5. Repeat Steps 3 and 4 to add additional sort levels, except in step 3, click the left side of the last sort level added before clicking Copy Level.

6. Click OK. Excel rearranges the table's rows in the color order you specified.

Part 12

Goal Seeking and What-If Analysis

What-if analysis refers to the process of changing one or more input cells and observing the effects on formulas. An *input cell* is a cell that a formula uses. If a formula calculates a monthly payment amount for a loan, for example, the formula refers to an input cell that contains the loan amount. *Goal seeking* is the reverse process of what-if analysis. Goal seeking determines the value that an input cell requires to produce a result that you want in a dependent (formula) cell.

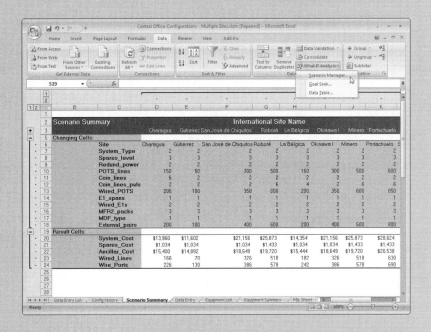

In this part . . .

✔ **Creating Data Input Tables**

✔ **Finding Input Values that Produce the Desired Output**

✔ **Using Scenario Manager**

Creating Data Input Tables

Using data tables is an excellent way to perform what-if analyses. Excel's Data Table feature enables you to set up a table to analyze data in the following ways:

- ✔ Calculate the results of one *or more* formulas for multiple values of a *single* input

- ✔ Calculate the results of a *single* formula for multiple values of *two* inputs

Creating a one-input table

A *one-input data table* displays the results of one or more *result* formulas for multiple values of a single *input cell*. For example, if you have formulas that calculate monthly loan payments, total loan payments, and total loan interest, you can create a data table that shows the results of these formulas for different interest rates. In this case, the interest rate cell is the input cell.

The following table describes how to set up a one-input data table.

Table Area	Description
Left column	Values for the single input cell
Top row	Formulas or references to result formulas elsewhere in the worksheet
Upper-left cell	Not used
Remaining cells	Results that Excel calculates

You can interchange the use of the left column and top row — that is, you can enter the values for the single input cell in the top row and enter the formulas or references in the left column.

The simplest way to explain how to set up a one-input data table is by using an example. Figure 12-1 shows is a table we set up using data from a loan-calculator model.

Figure 12-1

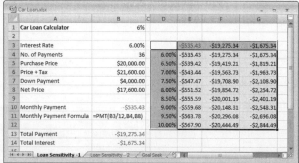

To create the table shown in Figure 12-1, follow these steps:

1. In an empty area of your worksheet (or on a separate sheet), enter the values that you want to use for the input cell. In Figure 12-1, we entered input values in cells D4 through D12.

2. Enter formulas or references to the formulas that you want Excel to calculate for the different input values. In Figure 12-1, we used formula references. Cell E3 contains the formula =**B10**, cell F3 contains the formula =**B13**, and so on.

3. Select the table range, including the input values in the left column and the formulas in the top row.

4. Click the Data tab on the Ribbon, click the What-If Analysis button, and choose Data Table from the menu. Excel displays the Data Table dialog box.

5. Specify the worksheet cell that you're using as the input value. In our example, cell B3 (Interest Rate) is the input cell. Because the values for the input cell are in a column (column D in this case), we used =**B3** in the Column input cell field. We left the Row input cell field blank.

   If the input cell values were in the top row (with the formulas in the left column), you would use the Row input cell field and leave the Column input cell field blank.

6. Click OK. Excel performs the calculations and fills in the table.

Remember: Excel uses an *array* formula that uses the TABLE function. Excel updates the table, therefore, if you change the cell references in the top row or plug in different values in the left column.

See also "Creating a two-input table," immediately following this section.

Creating a two-input table

A *two-input data table* displays the results of a single formula for various values of two-input cells. If you have a formula that calculates a monthly loan payment, for example, you can create a data table that shows the payment amount for various interest rates and loan amounts. The interest rate cell and the loan amount cell are the input cells.

The following table describes how to set up the two-input data table.

Table Area	Description
Left column	Values for the first input cell
Top row	Values for the second input cell
Upper-left cell	Reference to the single result formula
Remaining cells	Results that Excel enters

The simplest way to explain how to set up a two-input data table is by using an example. Figure 12-2 shows how we set up a table by using data from a loan-calculator model.

Figure 12-2

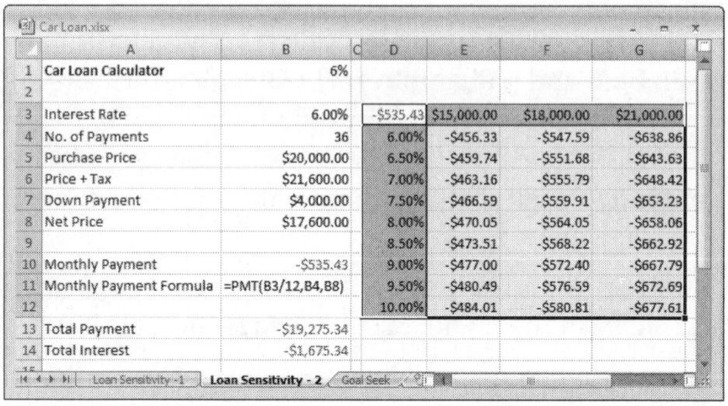

	A	B	C	D	E	F	G
1	Car Loan Calculator	6%					
2							
3	Interest Rate	6.00%		-$535.43	$15,000.00	$18,000.00	$21,000.00
4	No. of Payments	36		6.00%	-$456.33	-$547.59	-$638.86
5	Purchase Price	$20,000.00		6.50%	-$459.74	-$551.68	-$643.63
6	Price + Tax	$21,600.00		7.00%	-$463.16	-$555.79	-$648.42
7	Down Payment	$4,000.00		7.50%	-$466.59	-$559.91	-$653.23
8	Net Price	$17,600.00		8.00%	-$470.05	-$564.05	-$658.06
9				8.50%	-$473.51	-$568.22	-$662.92
10	Monthly Payment	-$535.43		9.00%	-$477.00	-$572.40	-$667.79
11	Monthly Payment Formula	=PMT(B3/12,B4,B8)		9.50%	-$480.49	-$576.59	-$672.69
12				10.00%	-$484.01	-$580.81	-$677.61
13	Total Payment	-$19,275.34					
14	Total Interest	-$1,675.34					

To create the table shown in Figure 12-2, follow these steps:

1. In an empty area of your worksheet (or on a separate sheet), enter the values that you want to use for the first input cell. In Figure 12-2, we entered the first input cell values in cells D4 through D12.
2. Enter the values that you want to use for the second input cell. In Figure 12-2, we entered the second input cell values in cells E3 through H3.
3. In the cell immediately above and to the left of the two input cells (upper-left cell), enter a formula or a reference to the formula that you want Excel to calculate for combinations of the two input values. In the figure, we used a formula reference. Cell D3 contains the formula **=B10**.
4. Select the table range, including the input values in the left column and the input values in the top row.
5. Click the Data tab on the Ribbon, click the What-If Analysis button, and choose Data Table from the menu. Excel displays the Data Table dialog box.
6. Specify the cell for the Row input cell. In the figure, the value in the Row input cell is **=B8**.
7. Specify the cell for the Column input cell. In the figure, the value in the Column input cell is **=B3**.
8. Click OK. Excel performs the calculations and fills in the table.

See also "Creating a one-input table," earlier in this part.

Finding Input Values that Produce the Desired Output

Excel's Goal Seek feature enables you to determine the value that a single input cell requires to produce a result that you want in a dependent (formula) cell. If you use the PMT function to calculate the monthly payment of a loan, for example, you may want to determine the loan amount for a specific monthly payment (given a fixed interest rate and payment term). You can adjust the cell that contains the loan amount manually until the formula that contains the PMT function provides the result you want, but using the Goal Seek feature is much faster:

1. Activate the worksheet that contains your formula.

2. Click the Data tab on the Ribbon, click the What-If Analysis button, and choose Goal Seek from the menu. Excel displays the Goal Seek dialog box.

3. Specify the formula cell to change (in the Set Cell text box), the value to change it to (in the To Value text box), and the input cell to change (in the By Changing Cell text box). The input cell must be referenced in your formula. See an example in Figure 12-3.

Figure 12-3

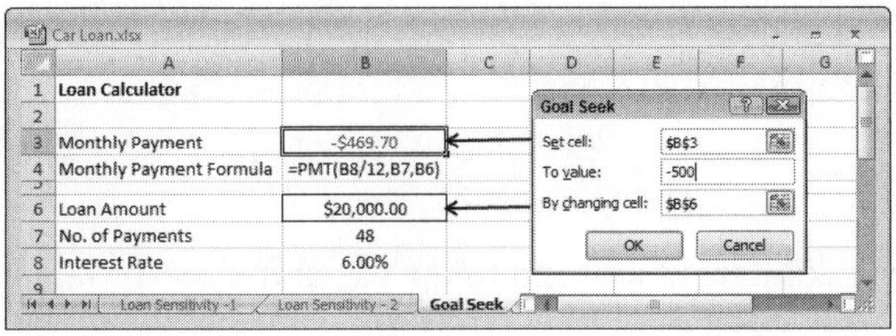

4. Click OK. Excel displays the solution in the worksheet and in the Goal Seek dialog box.

5. To restore your worksheet to the form that it was in before you initiated the Goal Seek command, click Cancel. Or to replace the original value with the found value, click OK.

Remember: Excel can't always find a value that produces the result that you're looking for. (Sometimes a solution doesn't exist.) In such a case, the Goal Seek status box informs you of that fact. If Excel reports that it can't find a solution, but you're pretty sure that one exists, try the following options:

✔ Change the current value of the changing cell to a value that is closer to the solution, and then reissue the command.

✔ Turn on Iterative Calculation and adjust the Maximum Iterations setting in the Formulas tab of the Excel Options dialog box (by clicking the Office button and clicking then Excel Options). Increasing the number of iterations makes Excel try other possible solutions. *See also* "Handling Circular References," in Part 7.

See also "Creating Data Input Tables," earlier in this part.

Using Scenario Manager

Excel's Scenario Manager feature makes it easy to automate your what-if models. You can store different sets of input values (known as *changing cells*) for any number of variables and give a name to each set. You can then select a set of values by name, and Excel displays the worksheet using those values. You can generate a summary report (in outline or PivotTable form) that shows the effect of various combinations of values on any number of result cells.

Creating a named scenario

To define a scenario, follow these steps:

1. Create your worksheet as usual, using input cells that determine the result of one or more formulas.

2. Click the Data tab on the Ribbon, click the What-If Analysis button, and choose Scenario Manager from the menu. Excel displays the Scenario Manager dialog box.

3. Click the Add button to add a scenario in the Add Scenario dialog box, as shown in Figure 12-4.

Figure 12-4

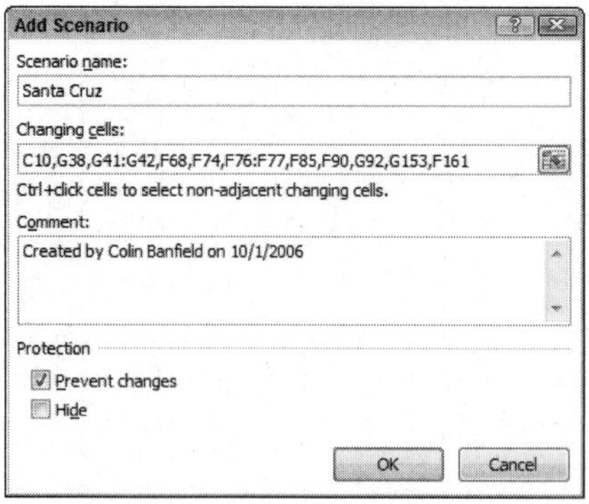

4. Complete the Add Scenario dialog box. The following list describes the settings in this dialog box:

- **Scenario Name:** The name for the scenario. You can give it any name you want.

- **Changing Cells:** The input cells for the scenario. You can enter the cell addresses directly or point to them. Multiple selections are possible, so the input cells don't need to be adjacent. Each named scenario can use the same set of changing cells or different changing cells.

- **Comment:** By default, Excel displays who created the scenario and the date that person created it. You can change this text, add new text to it, or delete it.

- **Protection:** The two Protection options (Prevent Changes and Hide) are in effect only if the worksheet is protected and the Edit Scenarios check box is deselected in the Protect Sheet dialog box. Prevent Changes protects a scenario from modification; Hide prevents the scenario from appearing in the Scenario Manager dialog box. *See also* "Protecting a Worksheet," in Part 3.

5. Click OK to display the Scenario Values dialog box.

6. Enter values for the changing cells in the appropriate text boxes.

7. Click the Add button to add the scenario.

8. Repeat Steps 4–7 for each additional scenario.

9. Click Close to close the Scenario Manager dialog box.

 TIP An excellent practice is to create names for changing cells to make the cells easier to identify in the Scenario Values dialog box. Names also help make scenario reports more readable. *See also* Part 6, "Creating and Using Names."

Remember: A scenario can have no more than 32 changing cells.

See also "Creating a scenario summary report," immediately following.

Creating a scenario summary report

After you define at least two scenarios, you can generate reports that summarize the scenarios by following these steps:

1. Click the Data tab on the Ribbon, click the What-If Analysis button, and choose Scenario Manager from the menu. Excel displays the Scenario Manager dialog box.

2. Click the Summary button.

3. Select the type of report, as follows:

   - Scenario summary: The summary report is in the form of an outline.

   - Scenario PivotTable: The summary report is in the form of a PivotTable. This option gives you more flexibility if you define many scenarios with multiple result cells.

4. In the Result Cells text box, specify the summary cells to include in the report.

5. Click OK. Excel creates a new worksheet to store the summary table.

 An excellent practice is to create names for the result cells, because Excel uses these names in the scenario summary reports that you create. The names help make your reports more readable. ***See also*** Part 6, "Creating and Using Names."

Remember: Result cells must be in the same worksheet as the changing cells.

See also "Creating a named scenario," earlier in this part, and "Creating a PivotTable Report," in Part 13.

Displaying a named scenario

As you view a scenario, Excel inserts the scenario's values into the changing cells in the worksheet. Formulas that depend on these cells are updated. To view a named scenario, follow these steps:

1. Click the Data tab on the Ribbon, click the What-If Analysis button, and choose Scenario Manager from the menu. Excel displays the Scenario Manager dialog box.

2. In the Scenarios list box, select the scenario.

3. Click Show. Excel updates the changing cells in the worksheet by using the scenario's values.

You can view as many scenarios as you want while the Scenario Manager dialog box is open. After you finish, click Close. Values for the last scenario viewed remain in the worksheet.

Part 13

Analyzing Data with PivotTables

A *PivotTable* report (or simply a *PivotTable*) is a dynamic table that organizes and summarizes data that exists in a tabular form. This manipulation enables you to view relationships, make comparisons, detect patterns and analyze trends among some of or all fields in your raw data.

In this part . . .

- ✔ **Creating and Formatting a PivotTable Report**
- ✔ **Filtering a PivotTable Report**
- ✔ **Grouping PivotTable Items**
- ✔ **Modifying a PivotTable's Structure**

Anatomy of a PivotTable

In contrast to a table, in which you present and analyze the details of your data, a PivotTable enables you to present and analyze your data in a summarized form. Moreover, a PivotTable (see Figure 13-1) enables you to view different dimensions of your summarized data in hierarchical levels of detail.

The following is a description of the elements in a PivotTable:

✔ **PivotTable Field List task pane:** Displayed after you indicate that you want to create a PivotTable from the source data. The task pane includes the field labels (column titles) from the source data and boxes that correspond to areas on the PivotTable.

Figure 13-1

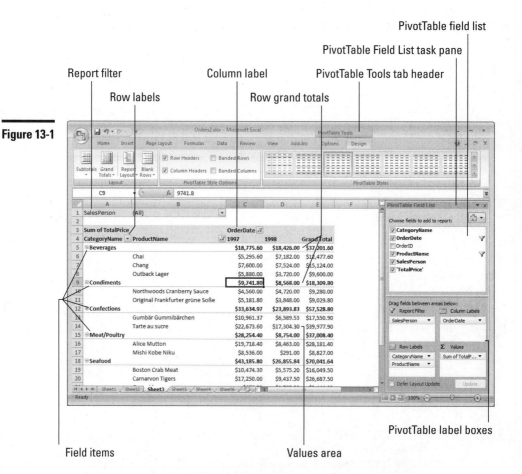

- **Row labels:** Fields that you want to summarize in rows.
- **Field Item:** An individual item in the row or column areas of the PivotTable.
- **Column labels:** Fields that you want to summarize in columns.
- **Values:** The data being summarized (for example, Sum of TotalPrice).
- **Report filter:** One or more of the fields in the Field List task pane used to filter the PivotTable report.

Remember: To construct a PivotTable report, at a minimum you need to choose a field to summarize in the data area and one field for either the row or column area. Your choices depend on how you want to view your data.

Remember: The source data that feeds the PivotTable is held in an area of system memory known as a *PivotCache*. If you have sufficient memory and the source data comes from an external data source, you may able to create a PivotTable from source data that has more rows or columns than Excel supports. This is possible if after summarization, the data fits within Excel's row and column limits.

Changing the Summarization of a Value Field

When you add a numeric field to the Values area of a PivotTable, Excel uses the Sum function to summarize the data. If you add a text field to the Values area, Excel uses the Count function to summarize the text data. The Count function is the only way to summarize text data, but Excel provides several alternative options for summarizing numeric data. To select a different summarization function other than Excel's default, right-click within a numeric field in the values area of the PivotTable, choose Summarize Data By from the contextual menu, and then choose an option from the flyout menu. Excel displays the new summary for the selected field.

TIP

You can display different summarizations for the same numeric field in the PivotTable. For each new summarization, simply drag the field label from the field list in the task pane to the Values box (the Values box can have the same field multiple times). Each time you drag the field to the Values box, Excel adds the field to the values area of the PivotTable using the default summarization. To change the default, use the procedure outlined for changing the summarization.

Creating a PivotTable Report

The data for your PivotTable can come from an external data source (such as a database) or an Excel range or table. *See also* Part 11, "Working with Tables." Although you can create a PivotTable from an ordinary (non-table) worksheet range, using a table is preferable — if the table expands or shrinks, after you refresh the PivotTable the data for it is based on the new table range.

To create a PivotTable report from a table, follow these steps:

1. Move the cell pointer to any cell in the table.

2. Click the Insert tab on the Ribbon and then click the top part of the PivotTable button. Excel displays the Create Pivot Table dialog box and outlines the table's data area. Excel inserts the table name in the Table/Range box.

3. In the lower half of the dialog box, specify where you want to locate the PivotTable and then click OK. If you select the Existing Worksheet option, click the Location box and then click the cell in the worksheet that will be the upper-left corner of the PivotTable. Excel displays the PivotTable Field List task pane and the area on the worksheet that will hold the PivotTable. In addition, Excel displays PivotTable tools contextual tabs on the Ribbon.

4. In the Field List task pane, select the check boxes next to the field labels of the fields you want to include or drag the field labels to the boxes in the lower portion of the task pane. These boxes correspond to the label areas in the PivotTable where your selected fields will appear (see Figure 13-2).

If you select check boxes, Excel chooses the boxes in the lower portion of the task pane to place the field labels based on the following assumptions:

- Field labels for numeric fields (such as TotalPrice) are placed in the Values box.

- Field labels for non-numeric fields are placed in the Row Labels box.

To override Excel's default behavior, drag the field labels from the list in the top window to the appropriate boxes in the lower portion of the task pane.

After Excel places field labels in the boxes (or you drag the labels to the boxes manually), the field data appears in the appropriate PivotTable label areas on the worksheet. By default, field labels in the Values box sum the corresponding data that appears in the values area of the PivotTable.

Figures 13-1 and 13-2 demonstrate the hierarchical nature of summarizing data in a PivotTable and the relationship between the arrangement of the fields in the task pane and the worksheet display.

The ability to drag field labels within the task pane is new. Excel 2007 also provides +/- indicators next to each level header on the worksheet, allowing you to quickly expand or collapse a level of detail in the PivotTable summary. Furthermore, when you create a PivotTable in Excel 2007, Excel displays the PivotTable in the new Compact layout shown in Figure 13-2 by default. In the Compact Layout, the actual row and column labels (see Figure 13-1) are not displayed, so you can view more of a wide PivotTable in the workbook window.

Figure 13-2

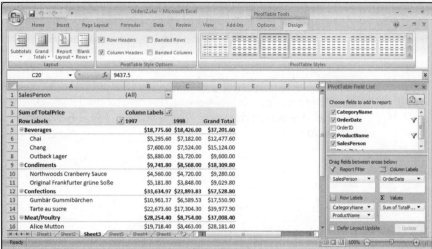

Filtering a PivotTable Report

In most ways, filtering a PivotTable is similar to filtering a table (see "Filtering Data in a Table," in Part 11). In the case of PivotTables however, you're filtering summarized data as opposed to a detailed dataset.

Filtering a PivotTable based on individual field items

Follow these steps to filter fields in your PivotTable based on individual field items:

1. Click the arrow on the header of the row or column field you want to filter. If you're using the Compact report layout, the individual field headings aren't shown but are represented by a Row Labels header (in the row area) and a Column Labels header (in the column area). Click the arrow on the Row Labels or Column Labels header. Excel displays the Sort and Filter menu. Figure 13-3 shows the Sort and Filter menu in the Compact Report Layout.

2. If you're using the Compact report layout, you must first choose the field you want to filter from the Select Field drop-down list in the Row Labels or Column Labels Sort and Filter menu. The lower portion of the menu displays the field items in a window. By default, Excel selects all items. If you want to display one or only a few entries, you can clear the Select All check box and select individually the items you want displayed. Alternatively, if you want to *hide* only a few items, clear the check boxes next to these items but do not clear the Select all check box.

Figure 13-3

3. Click OK. In the PivotTable, Excel displays the items you selected in Step 2 and hides all cleared items. Excel also adds a filter icon (a small funnel) on the field drop-down arrow and on the right of the field label in the task pane to indicate that a filter is applied to the field.

4. To filter additional fields, repeat Steps 2 and 3.

TIP If your PivotTable includes a report filter, you can select multiple items to display or filter by clicking the report filter drop-down arrow and selecting or clearing items from the menu. In the menu, make sure that the Select Multiple Items check box is selected.

Filtering a PivotTable based on field data type

EXCEL 2007
2007

Similar to tables, a field can be filtered by data type (that is value, label or date).

To filter a PivotTable field based on date, number, or label criteria, follow these steps:

1. Click the arrow on the field header of the field you want to filter. If you're using the Compact report layout, individual field headings aren't shown. In this case, click the arrow on Row Labels or Column Labels. Excel displays the Sort and Filter menu.

2. If you're using the Compact report layout, you must first choose the field you want to filter from the Select Field drop-down list in the Row Labels or Column Labels Sort and Filter menu. Above the field items window, choose the *datatype* Filters option (where *datatype* is Label, Number or Date, depending on the data type of the field you're filtering). Each row or column field in a PivotTable has a Value filter and either a Label or Date filter.

3. Choose a filter option from the flyout menu.

4. Complete the dialog box for the filter option and then click OK.

Pre-filtering a PivotTable

Excel 2007 allows you to filter fields from the source data before adding the fields to the PivotTable. This feature can be useful if you need to analyze a subset of the data in a large dataset (located in an external database, for example).

To filter a field before adding the field to the PivotTable, click the field label in the task pane's field list and follow the steps for "Filtering a PivotTable based on individual field items" or "Filtering a PivotTable based on field data type," previously in this section, depending on the type of filter you want to apply.

Clearing PivotTable filters

During your analysis of the data in a PivotTable, you may have applied multiple filters to one or more fields. You can manually remove the filters one by one, but Excel provides a quicker way to remove filters from your PivotTable:

✔ To clear filters from a single field, click the arrow on the field header of the field from which you want to remove filters (either on the PivotTable or the task pane field list). If you're using the Compact report layout, click the arrow on Row Labels or Column Labels. Then, from the Sort and Filter menu, choose Clear Filter From *fieldname*, where fieldname is the name of field whose filters you're clearing (for example, ProductName). If you're using the Compact report layout, you must first choose the field from which you want to remove the filters from the Select Field drop-down list in the Sort and Filter menu.

✔ To clear all filters in the PivotTable, click anywhere in the PivotTable, click the Sort & Filter button in the Ribbon's Home tab, and choose Clear from the menu.

Formatting a PivotTable Report

When you create a PivotTable, Excel applies a default style to the PivotTable. However, you can apply a different predefined style to the PivotTable or create a new style. You can also apply formatting based on the contents or a cell or a PivotTable field.

Applying a new style to a PivotTable

Follow these steps to apply a new predefined style to a PivotTable:

1. Click any cell in the PivotTable and then click the Design tab.

2. Select a new style from the PivotTable Styles gallery.

   You can scroll the gallery options by clicking the upper (scroll) arrows on the right side of the gallery, or you can display a drop-down grid by clicking the arrow below the scroll arrows. Preview a style by hovering the mouse pointer over the style.

3. In addition, or as an alternative, to Step 2, you can select style and display options from the PivotTable Style Options group. Check or clear the appropriate check boxes.

Remember: The styles you apply from the PivotTable Styles gallery are based on the theme applied to the workbook. Therefore, if you change the workbook theme, the applied PivotTable style and the gallery styles change to match the new theme. *See also* "Formatting with Themes," in Part 1.

Formatting based on data values

Formatting a PivotTable based on data values (conditional formatting) is similar to formatting a non-PivotTable cell or range based on the contents of the cell or range. *See:* "Formatting Based on the Contents of a Cell or Range," and "Formatting a Range using Visualizations," both in Part 8.

In earlier versions of Excel, you could apply conditional formatting to some or all cells in the values area of the PivotTable. However, the formatting was not applied at the field level, so if the PivotTable source data was updated with new information, Excel did not extend the conditional formatting to include the new data. In Excel 2007, after you select a cell or range of cells in the values area and apply a conditional formatting rule, a Formatting Options SmartTag (a small icon on the right of the selection) appears (see Figure 13-4).

Figure 13-4

OrderDate ↓		
1997	1998	Grand Total
$18,775.60	$18,426.00	$37,201.60
$5,295.60	$7,182.00	$12,477.60
$7,600.00	$7,524.00	$15,124.00
$5,880.00		
$9,741.80		
$4,560.00		
$5,181.80		
$33,634.97		
$10,961.37	$6,589.53	$17,550.90

Apply formatting rule to ...
- ◉ Selected cells
- ○ All cells showing "Sum of TotalPrice" values
- ○ All cells showing "Sum of TotalPrice" values for "ProductName" and "OrderDate"

Clicking the SmartTag provides the following options:

✔ Selected cells: This is the default option. Excel applies the conditional formatting to the selected cells only.

- ✔ All cells showing "Sum of *fieldname*" values, where *fieldname* is the name of a values field (for example, TotalPrice): Excel applies the conditional formatting to all cells showing Sum of *fieldname* values in the PivotTable, regardless of the field's hierarchical level, and includes subtotals and grand totals. If the subtotals or grand totals displays are turned on, this option is useful for summarizations that aren't sums (otherwise the subtotals and grand totals will skew any conditional formatting based on the range of values in the field). An example of a useful summarization for this option is "Average of *fieldname*."

- ✔ All cells showing "Sum of *fieldname*" values for *RowField* and *ColumnField*, where *fieldname* is the name of a values field (for example, TotalPrice), *RowField* is the name of a row field, and *ColumnField* is the name of a column field. Excel applies the conditional formatting to all cells showing Sum of *fieldname* values in the PivotTable for the row and column fields that correspond to the cells you selected for conditional formatting, and excludes subtotals. *ColumnField* is excluded from the option if the PivotTable doesn't include any column fields.

In the preceding list, we assume that the values field is summarized using the Sum function (Excel's default). The actual name on the option depends on the summarization function applied to the field. If the values are averaged, for example, the name will be "All cells showing "Average of *fieldname*" values.

Remember: If you select either of the last two options in the preceding list, after the PivotTable is refreshed, Excel extends the conditional formatting to include the new data.

Remember: Formatting is applied to a PivotTable in the following order: direct formatting (for example, formatting that you apply from the Font group in the Ribbon's Home tab) appears over PivotTable style formatting and conditional formatting appears over direct formatting.

Changing the number format of a PivotTable field

In creating a PivotTable report, Excel doesn't retain any special number formatting that you may have applied to your original data. If you apply a currency format to your source data, for example, and then use that data in the PivotTable, Excel doesn't retain the currency formatting in the PivotTable report.

To change the number format for a field in the PivotTable report, follow these steps:

1. Select any cell in the field in which you want to change the number format. Most often, you will use this option to change the number format in the values area of the PivotTable, but you can change the number formats of numeric or date fields in the row or column areas.

2. Right-click and choose Field Settings or Value Field Settings from the contextual menu (the name on the contextual menu depends on whether you're changing the number format of a row/column field or a values field). Excel displays the Field Settings or Value Field Settings dialog box.

3. Click the Number Format button. Excel displays the Format Cells dialog box.

4. In the Category list box, select a number format category and then select a format on the right side of the Format Cells dialog box.

5. Click OK to exit the Format Cells dialog box, and click OK again to exit the Field Settings or Value Field Settings dialog box.

A quick way to change the number format of cells in a values field is to right-click a cell in the field and choose Number Format to display the Format Cells dialog box.

Remember: After you apply a number format option using Field Settings, Value Field Settings, or Number Format options in the contextual menu, the formatting is applied to any new data that appears after you refresh the PivotTable. If you want to apply formatting (number, font, background, and so on) to only a cell or a group of cells, select the cell or range, right-click in the selection, choose Format Cells from the contextual menu, and make your selections in the Format Cells dialog box that appears.

Grouping PivotTable Items

A handy feature enables you to group specific items in a single field of a PivotTable report. If one of the fields in your source data consists of dates, for example, the PivotTable displays a separate row or column for every date. You may find that grouping the dates into months, quarters, or years is a more useful way to create a PivotTable report with a date field.

Remember: If you're grouping by date or number, the field you select for grouping can't have any blank items. Also, if you're grouping by date, all cells in the source data date field must carry one of Excel's recognized date or time formats.

Creating a date group

To create a date group PivotTable, follow these steps:

1. Right-click a cell in the date field that you want to group and choose Group from the contextual menu. Excel displays the Grouping dialog box (see Figure 13-5).

Figure 13-5

2. Select the grouping(s) you want. Note the following when selecting your grouping(s):

   - To select more than one grouping, click each grouping option in turn. Click a grouping option a second time to deselect it.

   - To group weekly or biweekly, select the Days option and specify 7 or 14, respectively, in the Number of Days box.

   - If you select a multiple days grouping and then select another grouping (for example, months, quarter, or years), Excel ignores the multiple days group because it's not possible to group across grouping boundaries. For example, if you attempt to group by week and by month, the weekdays can span across two months, so it's impossible to accommodate both groupings simultaneously.

3. In the dialog box, Excel automatically chooses the starting and ending dates for the group based on the range of dates in the PivotTable. To manually specify the starting date or ending date or both, clear the check box next to Starting At or Ending At and enter a new date in the text box. For example, if you're grouping by week and want to ensure that the week is grouped from Sunday to Saturday, in the Starting At text box, enter the Sunday date prior to Excel's selected starting date (unless Excel's starting date is Sunday).

4. Click OK. Excel creates the grouping(s).

If your date field covers multiple years and you elect to group by month or quarter or both, you should also include the Years grouping. If you don't include the Years grouping, each month or quarter will be summarized for all years, not for each year.

Creating a number group

If you create a PivotTable report and include a numeric field (or a text field that looks like a number) in the row or column areas of the PivotTable, you can create a number group. If, for example, you have a row field with a large number of order or invoice numbers, you might want to create a more Compact report. To create a number group, follow these steps:

1. Right-click a cell in the field in which you want to create a number group and choose Group from the contextual menu. Excel displays the Grouping dialog box.

2. In the dialog box, Excel automatically chooses the starting and ending numbers for the group. To manually specify the starting number or ending number or both, clear the check box next to Starting At or Ending At and enter a new number in the text box.

3. In the By text box, specify the number you want to group by.

4. Click OK. Excel creates the grouping.

Creating a text group

Excel allows you to create text groups. A text group might be useful, for example, if you want to group multiple states into sales territories. Follow these steps to create a text group:

1. Select the cells in the field that you want to group. If the items that you want to group aren't next to each other, you can make a multiple selection by pressing and holding Ctrl and then selecting the items that will make up the group.

2. Right-click any cell in the selection and choose Group from the contextual menu. Excel automatically creates the group with a generic title, such as *Group1*, *Group2* and so on.

3. To change the name of the group to something more meaningful, click the cell with the new group name a type a new name in the formula bar.

Modifying a PivotTable Report

A PivotTable is a special type of range, and (except for formatting) you can't manipulate it like a normal range. For example you can't insert or delete rows, edit results, or move cells. If you attempt to do so, Excel displays an error message. However, you can make certain modifications to the layout or structure of your PivotTable, some of which are described in this section.

Modifying a report layout

When you create a PivotTable, by default Excel uses the new Compact layout (see Figure 13-2) in which the actual row and column labels are hidden. This layout is useful if you have many fields in your report, because it minimizes horizontal space on the worksheet and can make reading the report easier. You can, however, use one of the following alternative layouts:

- ✔ Outline: This layout is similar to the Compact layout, except it displays the individual row and column headings (see Figure 13-1).

- ✔ Tabular: In this layout, the first item in a sublevel field appears not on a separate row (refer to Figure 13-1) but on the same row as its upper level (parent) field item.

To change the report layout, click anywhere in the PivotTable, click the Report Layout button in the Design tab, and choose a layout option from the menu.

Modifying a report structure

The power behind a PivotTable lies in its ability to display your summarized data in many dimensions by simply rearranging fields in the row, column, and values areas of the report and adding one or more report filters in the report filter area. Use any of the following techniques to rearrange the report structure to display your data differently:

- ✔ To add fields to the report, drag the field labels from the field list in the task pane to the appropriate label boxes below the field list. To remove a field from the report, either drag the field label off the appropriate label box or clear the check box next to the field name in the field list.

- ✔ To move fields between the row, column, and report filter areas of the report, drag the field labels between label boxes in the task pane.

- ✔ To rearrange levels in the row or column areas of the report, click and drag a field label in the row or column label box above or below the appropriate field labels in the same label box.

You can move fields also by clicking the field labels in the task pane label boxes and selecting a move option from the menu.

Displaying and hiding subtotals and grand totals

Sometimes, you may want to view your report with subtotals above or below a group or you may want to hide the subtotals display. Also, you may want to display grand totals in rows or columns only, or not at all. To change the display option for subtotals, click anywhere in the PivotTable, click the Subtotals button in the Design tab, and choose an option from the menu. To change the display option for grand totals, click anywhere in the PivotTable, click the Grand Totals button in the Design tab, and choose an option from the menu.

To turn off subtotals for only a single field, make sure that subtotals are turned on for the entire report, right-click an item in the field, and choose Subtotal *fieldname* from the contextual menu, where *fieldname* is the name of field whose subtotal you're turning off (for example, ProductName). To display subtotals for only one field, make sure that subtotals are turned off for the entire report, right-click an item in the field, and choose Subtotal *fieldname* from the contextual menu.

Expanding and collapsing field item levels

Expanding field item levels in your PivotTable report allows you to see sublevel item details in your report summary, and collapsing item levels allows you to hide sublevel details in your report summary.

Excel 2007 makes it easier for you to expand and collapse report levels than in earlier versions. Each higher-level field item has a +/- indicator button . Simply click the button to expand or collapse all sublevels below the field item. You can also expand or collapse to other levels of details as follows:

✔ To expand all sublevel items in a field, right-click an item in the field, choose Expand/Collapse from the contextual menu, and choose Expand Entire Field from the flyout menu. To collapse all sublevel items in a field, repeat the preceding but choose Collapse Entire Field from the flyout menu (see Figure 13-6).

Figure 13-6

✔ To expand a field item down to a specific sublevel, right-click an item in the field, choose Expand/Collapse from the contextual menu, and choose the field name from the bottom portion of the flyout menu.

Refreshing a PivotTable Report

If the source data that a PivotTable report uses changes, the PivotTable doesn't update automatically. You must refresh it manually. To refresh a PivotTable, click a cell in the PivotTable and then click Refresh on the Design tab or right-click anywhere in the PivotTable and choose Refresh from the contextual menu.

Glossary: Tech Talk

Absolute reference: A row, column, or cell reference in a formula, that doesn't change if you copy the formula to a different cell. An absolute reference uses one or two dollar signs, such as $A$15 (absolute cell reference), $A15 (absolute column reference), or A$15 (absolute row reference) for cell A15.

Active cell: The cell whose contents appear in the formula bar. You can enter information into the active cell or edit its contents.

Active workbook: The workbook containing the worksheet that contains the active cell. You make a workbook active by clicking the Switch Windows button in the Ribbon's Home tab and choosing the workbook from the menu.

Active worksheet: The worksheet containing the active cell. You make a worksheet active by clicking its tab.

Add-in: A file you load into Excel to provide additional commands or worksheet functions.

Argument: In a worksheet function, information (enclosed in parentheses) that provides details as to what you want the function to do.

Auditing: The process of tracking down and correcting errors in your worksheet.

AutoComplete: A tool that enables you to automatically complete a text or mixed text and number entry in a cell based on other entries already made in the same column.

AutoFill: A tool that enables you to fill in several types of data series in a range of cells.

AutoSum: A tool that enables you to enter common functions (such as sum, average, count, min, and max) quickly.

Cell: A single addressable unit in a worksheet that the intersection of a row and a column defines.

Cell comment: A comment that you attach to a cell.

Cell pointer: The dark border that surrounds the active cell. You move the cell pointer by using the mouse or the keyboard's arrow keys.

Cell reference: Identifies a cell by giving its column letter and row number. For example, C5 refers to the cell at the intersection of column C and row 5.

Cell tracers: Arrows that show the relationship between the active cell and its related cells (dependents or precedents or both).

Chart: A graphic representation of values in a worksheet. You can embed a chart on a worksheet or store it on a separate chart sheet in a workbook.

Chart element: Parts of a chart you can work with and modify, such as a data series, an axis, and gridlines.

Chart sheet: A type of sheet in a workbook that holds one or more charts. *See also* worksheet.

Check box: An option that you can either turn on by putting a check mark in a box (by clicking in the box) or turn off by clearing the box.

Circular reference: In a formula, a reference to the cell that contains the formula (either directly or indirectly). For example, if cell A10 contains =SUM(A1:A10), a circular reference exists because the formula refers to its own cell.

Column: Part of a worksheet that consists of 1,048,576 cells in a vertical arrangement. Each worksheet contains 16,384 columns.

Command group: A group of related commands on a Ribbon tab.

Conditional formatting: Formatting (such as color, bold text, bar, or icon) that you apply to a cell or range depending on the cell's or range's contents.

Contextual menu: The context-sensitive menu that appears after you right-click a cell, range, or object.

Contextual tab: One or more tabs that appears on the Ribbon after you insert or select an object, such as a chart, shape, table, or picture.

Data marker: A bar, area, dot, slice, or other symbol in a chart that represents a single data point or value that originates from a worksheet cell. Related data markers in a chart constitute a data series.

Data series: For a worksheet, refers to the values or text items that Excel fills into a range of cells after you use the AutoFill tool. For a chart, refers to related data points that you plot in the chart.

Data table: The data series represented in tabular form and placed directly below the horizontal axis in a chart.

Data validation: The process of ensuring that the user is entering data of the correct type into a cell.

Database: A systematic collection of information consisting of records (rows) and fields (columns). You can store a database in a worksheet (where it's known as a list) or in an external file.

Default workbook template: A template that you can use as the basis for new workbooks. This template has the name book.xlt, and you find it in your XLStart folder.

Dependent cell: A cell's dependents are formulas that reference the particular cell, either directly or indirectly.

Dialog box: An interactive window that appears in response to most commands. Excel uses a dialog box to get additional information from you so that it can carry out the command.

Dialog launcher: A command that launches a dialog box from within a Ribbon command group, a menu, or a gallery.

Double-click: To click the left mouse button rapidly twice.

Drag: To press and hold the left mouse button to move an object or extend a selection of cells.

Drag-and-drop: To use the mouse to grab a cell, range, or graphic object, move it, and drop it somewhere else.

Drop-down list box: A control that normally shows one option. If you click this control, a list drops down to show more options.

Embedded chart: A chart that Excel places on a worksheet (instead of it residing on a separate chart sheet).

Enhanced ScreenTip: Text that appears after you hover the mouse pointer over a tool that provides a short description (and sometimes a graphic) explaining how to use the tool.

Error value: A value that begins with a pound sign (#) appearing in a cell, signaling a formula error.

External data range: A range of data that you bring into a worksheet but that originates outside Excel, such as in a database, a text file or the Web.

Field: Data that contains a piece of information, such as a date or name.

Fill handle: The small, square object that appears at the lower-right corner of the active cell or a selected range of cells.

Filter: To hide rows in a range, table, or PivotTable such that only the rows that meet a certain criteria are visible.

Font: The typeface Excel uses for text and values.

Footer: A line of information that appears at the bottom of each printed page.

Formatting: The process of changing the appearance of cells, ranges, or objects.

Formula: An entry in a cell that returns a calculated result.

Formula AutoComplete: A feature that tries to anticipate what you're typing in a formula and presents a list of matched items.

Formula bar: The area of Excel, just below the Ribbon, that displays the contents of the active cell. You can edit the cell in the formula bar.

Function: A special keyword that you use in a formula (SUM, AVERAGE, ROUND, and so on) to perform a calculation.

Gallery: A control that presents a set of graphic choices, such as a particular formatting style (patterns, colors, and effects) or a predefined layout.

Goal seeking: The process of determining the value of an input cell that returns a specified value in a dependent formula.

Gridlines: Lines that delineate the cells in a worksheet. In a chart, gridlines are extensions of the tick marks on the axes.

Header: A line of information that appears at the top of each printed page.

HTML document: A document that you format for the Internet or an intranet by using special formatting codes.

Icon: A small picture that you can click with your mouse. (In this book, an icon is a small picture in the left margin that calls your attention to various types of information.)

KeyTip: Alphanumerical indicator that can appear on a Ribbon command and contain a single letter, a combination of two letters, or a number, indicating what to type to activate the command.

Legend: In a chart, the small box that describes the data series.

Link formula: A formula that uses a reference to a cell that a different workbook contains.

Live Preview: A feature that lets you see the effect that a formatting option will have on your selection before you commit to applying the option.

Locked cell: A cell that you can't change if the worksheet is protected.

Margin: The blank space outside the printing area on a page.

Maximize: To make a window as large as it can become.

Merged cells: Cells that you combine into one larger cell that holds a single value.

Minimize: To hide a window from view. You can restore the window by clicking its icon in the Windows taskbar.

Mixed reference: In a formula, a reference to a cell that is partially absolute and partially relative. A mixed reference uses one dollar sign, such as A$15 for cell A15. In this case, the column part of the reference is relative; the row part of the reference is absolute.

Mouse pointer: The object that you see move on-screen as you move your mouse. The mouse pointer often changes its shape, depending on what you're doing at the time.

Name box: A combination text and drop-down list box that resides below the Ribbon and to the left of the formula bar. You can use this box to define names of cells and ranges or to select a named cell or range.

Named range: A range to which you assign a name. Using named ranges in formulas makes your formulas more readable.

Nested function: A function that uses another function as one of its arguments.

Noncontiguous range: A range of cells that don't lie in a single rectangular area. You select a noncontiguous range by pressing Ctrl as you select cells.

Number format: The manner in which a value appears in Excel. You can format a number to appear with, for example, a percent sign and a specific number of decimal places. The number format changes only the appearance of the number, not the number itself.

Office Clipboard: A feature in Microsoft Office that enables you to copy up to 24 items at a time for pasting into any Office application.

Office Menu: The menu you use to perform file-related operations (such as open, save, and print) and that provides access to Excel's options.

Operator: In a formula, a character that represents the type of operation you intend to perform, such as + (plus sign), / (division sign), and & (text concatenation).

Operator precedence: The order in which Excel performs operations in formulas.

Option button: *See* Radio button.

Page break: A dashed line that appears on-screen to tell you where the pages break as you print the worksheet.

Page Break Preview mode: An editable view that superimposes page numbers and page breaks on the worksheet. You can drag the page breaks to move them.

Page Layout View mode: An editable view that allows you to view and work with printing options such as headers and footers, margins, and page orientation.

Pane: One part of a worksheet window that's split into either two or four parts.

PivotTable report: A table that summarizes information that a worksheet table or external database contains.

Pointing: The process of selecting a range by using the mouse. If you need to enter a cell or range reference into a dialog box, you can either enter it directly or point to it in the worksheet.

Precedent cell: A cell that a formula cell refers to. A single formula can have many precedent cells, and the precedents can be direct or indirect.

Print area: One or more ranges of cells that you designate to print if you don't want to print the entire worksheet.

Print title: One or more rows or columns or both that appear on each page of printed output.

Protected workbook: A workbook that prevents users from making changes to workbook elements and optionally prevents users from viewing and editing the workbook.

Protected worksheet: A worksheet in which you restrict elements (such as cells with formulas) from user access.

Quick Access toolbar: A toolbar that sits above the Ribbon and provides quick access to commands.

Radio button: One of a group of buttons in a dialog box. You can select only one button in the group at any time. Also known as *option button*.

Range: A collection of two or more cells.

Range finder: The colored frame that indicates cells that a formula references or that a chart uses. You can grab and move the frame to change the formula or chart series references.

Recalculate: To update a worksheet's formulas by using the most current values.

Redo: To reverse the effects of an undo operation.

Relative reference: In a formula, a reference to a cell that changes (in a relative manner) if you copy the formula to a different cell. A relative reference doesn't use dollar signs (as does an absolute reference or a mixed reference).

Restore: To return a window (either the Excel window or a workbook window) to its previous size.

Ribbon: Excel 2007's command interface, which consists of a series of tabs, each containing a variety of commands grouped according to function.

Ribbon group: A group of related commands on a Ribbon tab.

Rich menu: A menu with options that have an illustrative graphic, the command name, and sometimes a description of what the command does.

Right-click: To click the right mouse button.

Row: Part of a worksheet that consists of 16,384 cells in a horizontal arrangement. Each worksheet contains 1,048,576 rows.

Scenario: A specific set of values for input cells. You assign each scenario a name, and you can display the scenario using the Excel scenario manager.

ScreenTip: Text that pops-up on-screen to provide information on a selected element (such as a toolbar button or a dialog box option). Unlike Enhanced ScreenTips, the standard ScreenTip does not describe how to use the selected element.

Scroll bar: One of two bars (on the right and bottom of a workbook window) that enable you to scroll quickly through the worksheet by using the mouse.

Selection: The active item. A selection can consist of a cell or range, part of a cell's content, part of a chart, or one or more graphic objects.

Sheet: One unit of a workbook, which can consist of a worksheet or a chart sheet. You activate a sheet by clicking its sheet tab.

SmartTag: A button that appears when the user needs it (such as when a user makes an error in a formula or applies certain commands to a selection) and provides the options needed to change the action or error.

Sort: To rearrange the order of rows in a range or table or the field items in a PivotTable, based on the contents of one or more range or table columns or PivotTable fields. You can sort in ascending or descending order.

Split button: A button that consists of two parts. One part allows you to access a command directly and the other part (with an arrow) presents a menu.

Spreadsheet: A generic term for a product such as Excel that you use to track and calculate data. People often use this term to refer to a worksheet or a workbook.

Status bar: The line at the bottom of the Excel window that shows the status of several items, houses the zoom and view controls, and displays messages.

Style: A combination of formatting characteristics, such as font, font size, and indentation, that you name and store as a set. If you apply a style, Excel applies all the formatting instructions in that style at one time.

Table: A specially designated range in Excel that consists of a header row, data rows, and a totals row.

Task pane: A window that enables you to perform certain tasks quickly and easily (such as pasting items that you first copy to the Office Clipboard) or that contains a list of fields you add to a PivotTable.

Template: A file that you use as the basis for a new workbook or chart.

Text attribute: A format that you apply to a cell's contents, such as bold, underline, italic, or strikethrough.

Theme: A combination of fonts, colors, and effects that, when applied to workbook elements such as cells, charts, tables, and PivotTables, provides a consistent look among the elements.

Title bar: The colored bar at the top of every window. To move a non-maximized window, drag its title bar.

Undo: To reverse the effects of the last command (or as many as 100 of the previous commands) by clicking the Undo button on the Quick Access toolbar (or by pressing Ctrl+Z).

Value: A number that you enter into a cell.

Visualization: A data bar, a color scale, or an icon set that allows you to compare the relative values in a range visually.

Watch window: A window that enables you to view cells and their formulas, especially if the cells are out of view.

What-if analysis: The process of changing one or more input cells and observing the effects on one or more dependent formulas. The Excel Scenario Manager and Data Input table features enable you to easily perform what-if analyses.

Window: A container for an application or a workbook. You can move and resize windows.

Workbook: The name for a file that Excel uses. A workbook consists of one or more sheets.

Worksheet: A sheet in a workbook that contains cells. Worksheets are the most common type of sheet. *See also* chart sheet.

Workspace file: A file that contains information about all open workbooks: their size, arrangement, and position. You can save a workspace file and then reopen it to pick up where you left off.

Zoom: To expand or contract the size of the text appearing in a window. Zoom in to make text larger, and zoom out to make text smaller so that you can see more.

Index

protected, 27–29, 211
saving, 29–32
saving as template, 33–34
switching between open workbooks, 32
worksheet tabs, coloring, 39
worksheets
active, 38, 207
adding to workbook, 38
column headers for, 4
column headings in, freezing, 40–41
columns in, definition of, 208
columns in, deleting, 54–55, 66–67
columns in, hiding, 128
columns in, inserting new columns, 66–67
columns in, maximum number of, 2
columns in, selecting, 72
columns in, unhiding, 129
columns in, width of, changing, 130
columns in, width of, too narrow, 124
copying, 39–40
copying cells to, 52
definition of, 2, 213
deleting, 40
display modes for, 137–138
full-screen view of, 48
grouping, 41–42
hiding, 42–43
maximum size of, 2
moving, 43
moving cells to another worksheet, 68–69

moving cells within worksheet, 67–68
name of, changing, 38–39
name of, inserting in header or footer, 144
names applied across multiple worksheets, 93
names applied only to worksheet and not workbook, 92
navigating with keyboard, 7–8
navigating with mouse, 5
printing, 150
protected, 44–45, 211
publishing to Web page, 45–46
references to cells or ranges in other worksheets, 85–86
row headers for, 4
row headings in, freezing, 40–41
rows in, definition of, 211
rows in, deleting, 54–55, 66–67
rows in, height of, changing, 130–131
rows in, hiding, 128, 209
rows in, inserting new rows, 66–67
rows in, maximum number of, 2
rows in, selecting, 72
rows in, unhiding, 129
selecting multisheet (3-D) ranges, 72–73
splitting into panes, 46–47
ungrouping, 42
unhiding, 43
zooming, 48

workspace files
definition of, 32, 213
opening, 33
saving, 33
wrapping text, 115

X

`.xl*` **files, 26**
`.xla` **files, 30**
`.xlam` **files, 30**
`.xlb` **files, 30**
`.xls` **files, 30**
`.xlsb` **files, 30**
`.xlsm` **files, 26, 30**
`.xlsx` **files, 26, 30**
`.xlt` **files, 30**
`.xltm` **files, 30**
`.xlw` **files, 30**
xml files, saving workbooks as, 31

Y

years. *See* **dates and times**

Z

zooming, 4, 48, 213